Recovering Your Sacredness

Ancestral Teachings For Today's Living

JERRY TELLO

Sueños Publications LLC

Edited by: Frank Acosta, Susanna Armijo,
Emilio Tello, Renee Tello Spencer, Diane Lopez Wilson
Cover and Book design by: Diane Lopez Wilson,
Renee Tello Spencer

3129 Hacienda Blvd # 396
Hacienda heights, CA. 91745
JerryTello.com
SueñosPublicationsLLC.com

Printed in the United States of America
First printing 2018
ISBN 978-0-9993172-2-8

CONTENTS

*Front Cover: "The Sacred feathers are shared
to carry our healing prayers to the Creator."

ACKNOWLEDGEMENTS

- To the creator, who knows I am still learning, yet everyday grandfather sun shines the light to let me know that I have another chance to learn, grow, heal, and share. For that, I give gratitude.

- To the sacred universe: mother earth, grandfather sun, brother wind, sister water, grandmother moon, the plants, animals, four legged, creepy crawlers, winged and all my relations, I give thanks.

- For all the ancestors that have passed down these sacred ways, customs, and ceremonies, so that we may have the genetic memory to draw from our true ancestral ways, I give thanks.

- For all the women, especially my mother and grandmothers, my life companion Susanna, the comadres, and the lineage of women in my family; the givers of life for nurturing and reinforcing the sense of unconditional love and honor. And for all the women leaders and healers who have taught me, and have been patient with us men, allowing us time to heal, I give thanks.

- For all the men, my father and grandfathers, my uncles, brothers, the National Compadres Network, and compadres that have guided and taught me, picked me up and allowed me to teach them as well, I give thanks.

- For the children, especially Marcos, Renee, and Emilio, who I believe chose me and allowed me the opportunity to be their father, and guided me through many lessons along the way. For the honor of being a father and now a grandfather to Amara, Naiya, Greyson and Harrison; and for Paloma, Tenaya, Matt and Krystal who have blessed my life, and all those others from whom I've learned and am still learning. To those children, and all the children that I have been blessed to work with and who see me as their spiritual father, their uncle or grandfather, I give thanks.

♦ For all the maestras/os de los tradiciones, circulo of Calmecac and all the teachers and healers that have healed and taught me, have given me a chance to learn, and entrusted these teachings to me, I give thanks.

♦ For all the people who have trusted me with their story, their pain, and shame and through these journeys have gifted me their medicine, prepared me, and assisted me to fulfill my sacred purpose, I am so grateful.

♦ For you who have chosen to go on this journey of learning and healing with me, I give thanks.

♦ Finally, I very humbly ask for permission from all the ancestors, elders and all my relations to share these teachings, in a good way, recognizing that  they are not mine, but they are only one person's reflection of the sacredness. And if these teachings can help anyone, you or your relations, then the sacred circle of life continues and life goes on in a good way. I am truly grateful.

INTRODUCTION

*"I see a time of seven generations, when
all the colors will gather under the sacred
tree of life and the whole earth will
become one circle again."*

-CRAZY HORSE

In every healthy community, village, or barrio, historically and traditionally, there was a sacred tree where individuals, families, and the community as a whole would gather. The tree had its roots connected to the sacred elements of the universe: the earth, the sun, water, wind and grandmother moon. These elements connected generations of energy and life, serving as the symbolic focal point, rod of life, or spiritual altar.

Although ancient, the ever-present energy of those same roots continues today. The place of the tree provided a common fundamental bond, serving as the reference point from which a person, family, or community gained clarity of purpose, values, healing, and strength. Today, that gathering may take place in a sweat lodge, hogan, church, synagogue, community center, the home of the community healer/leader, or in the sacredness of nature. It was then the responsibility of each person and family to take the spirit of the rooted teachings and traditions into their homes, and instill this connection of sacredness within themselves and the members of their own family.

Based on this tradition, many families have a spiritual altar, or sacred space, in their homes with pictures or other spiritual objects with meaning, to remind them of the sacred teachings of their ancestors. The altar is a living symbol intended to assist in maintaining balance and keeping the connection and harmony with all of one's relations.

Gathering in Circles, Ceremony, Traditions, and Customs

It was for these reasons that families and communities increasingly understood that in order to survive and grow, they needed to continually be re-grounded in their sacred roots, their authentic history, and the positive principles of life. People have always gathered around the sacred tree or in sacred places, in circles, mirroring nature, as a way of honoring and keeping in harmony with these principles. In circles, and through positive ceremonies, traditions, and customs, the principles and values were taught, reinforced, and strengthened. The sacred principles provided the way for the individual, the family, and the community to survive through difficult times and not lose focus on one's greater purpose. The ceremonies and traditions also assured that life affirming values and principles were taught, maintained and passed on from generation to generation in a sacred way. And when one did stray from this sacredness, there was a welcoming, safe place to re-root oneself.

Various tribes and subgroups of indigenous people from around the world have their own interpretations of cultural principles and ceremonies based on the particular way of their rooted, ethnic tree, or spirit. Regardless of point of origin, it has been found that ethnic-centered people of all roots continue to gather in circles. Men, women, family, and communities gather to pray, to strengthen, center, re-balance, maintain harmony, and to re-root themselves in the principles of their sacred gathering/healing tree. With this understanding, we begin.

Almost universally, indigenous people recognize that all of creation has its origin from a spiritual place that gives life. The seed of a tree that goes way back and connects all of us to a genetic memory of wholeness: a wholeness that calls to us throughout our lives, especially in times of darkness and struggle. Despite this, we have all, at some point, found ourselves in that place of darkness— a state of imbalance that leaves us wondering how to get back to that place of health, harmony and fulfillment. For some, at times, the darkness lasts so long that we wonder if we can ever get back. For others, the journey back is so prolonged, lonely and painful, that we forget what balance really feels like. In that state of prolonged imbalance, one may begin to believe that this sense of disorientation, distortion, and darkness is normal. So, it is especially for those in the midst of the darkness and protracted time of aimlessness and hopelessness that these reflections and teachings are offered. Because when we get to that state of being, we tend to forget what health, wholeness and sacredness is. Without that feeling of wholeness, the thought of one being sacred or having a sacred purpose is not even a consideration. For this reason, this writing of *Recovering Your Sacredness* is offered to all, with a prayer of thanksgiving– from one who was/is a recipient of guidance, healing, and counsel, rooted in sacred medicine. The offerings herein are ancestral teachings of the circle of life that gives back. Like the Ollin– the interconnected movement, which returns what has been given in order for the genetic memory of the ancestors, of peace, healing and wholeness to continue. At the same time, I have attempted to offer and respectfully translate those sacred teachings into traditions and processes that can be integrated and applied to the issues and needs of today's spiritually and culturally diverse society. And although I have drawn on a number of my Mesoamerican indigenous teachings, I have purposely stayed away from describing or prescribing particular indigenous teachings and practices. This is in order to not disrespect the traditional way of learning, by walking under the  guidance of an elder. I have also purposely not delved deeply into explanations of the indigenous teachings or described indigenous practices in order to respect the spiritual ways of various traditions. This is especially important in a society that promotes and allows you to buy, order or become anything online, even a healer, shaman or minister. On the contrary, these teachings are to awaken and acknowledge your rooted, sacred-self. What I do lift up are practical processes and suggestions, through guidance and reflection, that will allow each of you to identify and build your own traditions, based on your own sacred identity.

With that in mind, I invite you to continue your journey toward a sacred place of harmony and interconnectedness. Let us join together as we journey to that sacred place of wholeness – a place where you can uncover, discover and recover your sacredness and your sacred purpose.

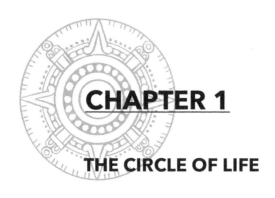

CHAPTER 1

THE CIRCLE OF LIFE

"Suddenly all my ancestors are behind
me. 'Be still,' they say. 'Watch and listen.
You are the result of the love of
thousands.'"

-LINDA HOGAN

As part of this sharing, I offer a variety of teachings that have come through my own life journey. Other lessons offered here have come while giving counsel and support to others. And some of these teachings are lessons that have been gained from challenges or blessings, in which we learn to fall, get up, and be guided to continue living... and hopefully grow from these experiences.

The learning begins with the blessing of one's birth, but many believe it truly started 7 generations before. But in the circle of life that begins with the birth of a child, when two people have come together - sometimes planned, sometimes not - male and female energies meet and they are blessed with a sacred moment in which the Creator, ancestors, and all the spirits say that a new life will enter this world; and a miracle happens.

And when that miracle of a child is born, the circle of life and life's lessons continue - for the child, for the parents, for the ancestors and for all their relations. This path we walk is all about life's circles; the sacred circle of life and the spiritual

energy that comes from the Creator, handed down through the ancestors, all our relations, and life's experiences. At the same time, each of us has our own journey, lessons and

challenges to embrace, giving us teachings to pass on to our own children and the subsequent generations that follow. Thus, the circle continues.

"The circle has healing power. In the circle, we are all equal. When in the circle, no one is in front of you. No one is behind you. No one above you. No one is below you. The sacred circle is designed to create unity. The hoop of life is also a circle. On this hoop, there is a place for every species, every race, every tree and every plant. It is this completeness of life that must be respected in order to bring about health on this planet."

-DAVE CHIEF, OGLALA LAKOTA

We also come to understand that life is about duality. As there is no night without day, or day without night. And each of us live, at times, in the light and other times, in the darkness. But every day we wake up in the morning and the Creator blesses us with Grandfather Sun to remind us that enlightenment is within us and is available to us every day.

Each day we get a new opportunity to learn, to shed, and to give blessings. Just as night follows day, we are reminded that there is a duality in the world - the lightness and darkness. And darkness is not necessarily negative or bad but rather, it represents the reflection, El Otro Yo, or opposite end of the light. And although some of us are afraid of the dark, the reality is there are certain lessons we can only learn in the dark. Only in the dark of night can we see the beautiful stars and moon; and if we are willing to face the dark, other magical teachings and experiences are then revealed. But at one time or another, we all have been wounded in the dark. And some of us were wounded so severely, that we are afraid of facing the dark secrets and pain of those experiences. Out of that fear of darkness comes the cycles of pain, shame, abuse, addiction, and fear, which are the cycles of imbalance and disconnectedness that stagnate many of us and sometimes hold us frozen. And these cycles can pull us away from our true selves, from our sacred relationships, and push us to treat others and ourselves in hurtful, harsh, criticizing, and painful ways. It is in the shadow energy of these cycles that sometimes harmful words and thoughts come out of people's mouths and minds, our own and others', pushing us to judge and criticize. And in doing so, this contributes to the disconnection, or fear of never being able to live at peace again. When one feels scared like this, they no longer feel sacred. They may become so afraid that they are going to be hurt or shamed again that they lose their connection with their own sacredness and with others as well.. And when that happens, a fear-based cycle of life takes on an energy that is larger than life itself, which begins to engulf one's total spirit. As this scenario continues, pain and fear begin to fester within. Those patterns then become integrated into one's heart and mind leaving them no longer knowing who they really are or who they are meant to be.

"When a person feels SCARED,

they no longer feel SACRED."

-JERRY TELLO

Unfortunately, as these negative cycles gain momentum, we may also begin practicing the same harmful patterns of abuse and disconnectedness on ourselves, and subconsciously upon others. We become self-critical, as our inner voice turns harsh and self-doubting. We may close off from healthy relationships; fearful, untrusting and no longer feeling worthy or sacred. In times like these, it is easy to forget who we really are, living life merely existing, instead of truly living.

"To live is the rarest thing in the world.

Most people exist, that is all."

-OSCAR WILDE

When we get stuck in this state of darkness and fear, it can pull us down so deep that it affects our total being, disturbing our sleep, thoughts, mood, health and our entire outlook on life. We then begin to just go through the motions of life, as opposed to living life in true movement.[1] In motion we continue asking the same "why?" questions, whether they get answered or not. "Why did this happen to me? Why did they treat me so badly? Why is my life so messed up? Why do people treat me this way? Why do I sabotage myself?" In essence, being stuck or depressed in life's journey. And if we are asking the wrong questions, we usually come up with the wrong answers, or no answers at all.

These patterns then draw us further away from our own sacredness, our connection to the Creator and our sense of true movement. What makes it more difficult is that our longing to be connected is so strong that in our wounded state, we have a tendency to surround ourselves with others who have similar patterns and who make us feel the same way over and over again. It is in those times that we forget to pray, forget our traditions and ceremony, and our healing ways. In essence, we lose our true self. Or we may participate in ceremonies or spirituality rituals, but not live these teachings every day, thus living a false life which brings more feelings of hopelessness and shame. In these shadow times we tend to stay away from the very people that know our truth and/or can help us to find our healing

---

[1] There is a difference between living in motion, and being in movement. Motion is just going around and around, occupying time and space, but staying stuck whether it's good for us or not. Movement is interconnected growing in your sacred purpose.

path back to our sacredness. To contribute to this disconnection, we live in a technologically based society that has given us an abundance of ways, through computers, media and pseudo-remedies, to occupy our time and falsely-connect us, as a way to fill the void. Technology seductively then demands more and more of our time thus leaving very little time or space for healing, growth and true interconnected development and thrusts us into a survival mode.

The thing about survival though is that it is not true growth. It is just that, *survival*. And it sets us up as victims in our own wounded stories, telling and living the same tale over and over again, and perpetuating the same cycles. Unfortunately, individual cycles can manifest into community and societal cycles, which are seen in many communities today.

But even in the darkest of places, it only takes a small glimmer of light, a simple teaching, a hug, a small prayer, or a sacred song to bring the enlightenment that opens a window of hope, which can transform our reality. It all depends on if we are open to the light, to the teaching, and whether we are ready to take the journey back to our sacred selves. Life presents these glimmers of light sometimes in the most simple of ways and, at times, when we least expect them.

I remember I was visiting with some very good friends who brought their daughter, Leela, over to the Sacred Circles Center in Whittier, California, where we offer teachings and healings. This little, precious girl was sitting with her parents and me in a room as we were discussing what was going on with each of us and sharing some very heavy burdens. In the room, there was a box of tissues, which we keep handy for people who need them as they are sharing their life's challenges. As we were talking, this little girl took a tissue out of the box and began to tear it into shreds, throwing it up in the air and laughing. The torn pieces were falling like snowflakes. Leela then threw some shredded pieces on her head and then on us. She threw it on me and I threw it back to her. She threw it to her dad, and he threw it back to her, and she was just playing. Pretty soon we all started laughing, as the energy had shifted in the room. As I watched this happen, I couldn't help but see the wonder in the moment.

This little girl transformed the tissues, which were normally present to wipe away people's tears, into something that brought joy. Her playing this little game brought a glimmer of light. She drew us out of the darkness, tears, and talking about the problems, into laughter and genuine joy. In the innocence of a child, she pointed out to us the duality of life - that even in the darkness and pain, when we get stuck and frozen in cycles of fear, can come a transformative moment, insight or blessing that can draw us back to the sacred duality. With the simplest of experiences, we can be released from the fear and depression, and experience a sacred moment. The questions then become, "Are we open to the light and will we seize the blessing by shifting with it? Are we willing to move with the light by doing our work to break the cycles, and commit to a life based on true sacred movement? Or, have we become so accustomed to darkness that we indirectly choose to remain there?"

The essence of the lessons presented here are to awaken us so that we will can acknowledge these moments and insights, which can shift our experiences so that we can return to the sacred path of fulfilling our sacred purpose. Although it may take work anytime we choose to face our sacred darkness, we are brought closer to our sacredness and closer to a connection with the Creator. Simultaneously, these teachings can also allow us to make peace with the baggage and the cycles of fear, pain, shame and disconnectedness that have walked with us in our lives, and transform them into medicine and *sacred circle of life teachings*.

I have found that the circle of life teachings are practiced in relationships by cultures across the world and can be the medicine for those who are stuck, wounded, or scared, in the shadows of life and the painful cycle of life experiences. It is these lessons and challenges that come to us through the various stages of life, beginning with *childhood*, where rooted teachings are planted. As we cross the *adolescent* bridge, physiological, emotional, mental and spiritual experiences bring an entire new series of teachings. Moving to the third phase of life, *adulthood*, we carry the sacredness or woundedness[2], and are given the additional responsibility to guide others. If we carry these unhealed wounds into adulthood, the brokenness can be passed onto subsequent generations. Finally, in the fourth stage of elderhood - it is the phase of sharing unconditional love and the wisdoms of life with the next generation. However, if an elder is wounded, the wounded elder's teachings can put in motion an inter-generational sharing of disconnectedness and pain that can have a profound effect on all for a long time to come. In every phase of life, there are teachings, so many that it could fill infinite volumes.

---

[2] Woundedness - The state of being engulfed by one's own wounds.

For now, we will focus on the most essential of those teachings, the rooted-tree teachings of childhood, because when the tree is well rooted, it can grow and sustain itself through even the toughest of times. It is also the phase of our lives where much of the confusion and woundedness begin. When the roots are not solid, the tree will always be vulnerable. When we do not receive the sacred root teachings in childhood, and instead receive teachings that are distorted, imbalanced, or shadowed, we will search our entire lives for a deeper truth or connection and feel a void, knowing in our spirit that something is missing. We may not even know what we are looking for, but the spirit always knows when something isn't right or is missing. In fact, many of us know of people who are 30, 40, 50 or older, who continue to throw tantrums the way a toddler would, who are still afraid of the dark or of being abandoned and cling to anything or anyone that crosses their path, like that of a dependent child or fearful teenager.

"You are either drawn by wisdom or pushed by pain. Either way, you will have to move."

-*CAROLINE MYSS*

So, if we didn't receive the essential rooted teachings of childhood and instead experienced the wounded side of life's lessons, at some point our spirit will search to try to heal. If misguided, we may look to substitute the need for these teachings in people, relationships, and perhaps eventually in food, alcohol, substances, work and/or other activities. And when disconnectedness, shame, neediness, or fear of rejection become our motivation for living, we end up in wounded relationships, settling for less than what is truly fulfilling, and/or stuck in a pattern of despair. It is for these reasons that we must return to the rooted lessons, because they are the basis for our growth and healing; and the very same teachings that children, the miracles of life, come into the world seeking and needing.

Interestingly enough, it is these teachings that are essential to a child's healthy development, and is the very same medicine that is needed as we get older, in order to heal the wounds in our lives. If we receive the rooted, sacred teachings early on, although adolescence may be a challenge, the resiliency of the rooted teachings will carry us through and prepare us to draw ourselves more towards the sacred, in everything we do. They will push us toward the values that guide us to make choices that keep us in balance. The hope is that everyone can move to adulthood to fulfill their life purpose and spend their elder years in joy and dignity, prepared to take on the responsibility of sharing those teachings with the next generation.

Our ultimate wish is that the cycles of life's wounds, sometimes generations old, will be healed; that the pain of the cycles and the energy of negative forces will be lessened so that the next generation will carry less burdens of pain, fear, self-destruction and disconnection, and more sacred teachings, of interconnectedness, joy and blessings.

CHAPTER 2

BEGINNING THE JOURNEY

"Movement toward your sacredness is the medicine that changes a person's physical, emotional, mental and spiritual well-being."

JERRY TELLO

For hundreds of millennia, individuals, families, communities, and societies have come together in various ways using the traditions of their ancestors to search for strength, attempting to stay healthy and live their lives in a good way. The traditional ways of various cultures prepare one to face the struggles and issues that sometimes threaten the very essence of one's life's journey. But even in difficult times, when there seems to be no hope for revitalization, a way always reveals itself. At one time or another, all of us have encountered similar episodes of challenges in our lives. The questions become: "How do we see these challenges? Are we prepared to recognize these challenges as an essential part of our journey? Or do we feel burdened by the struggles, feeling victimized and stuck in the challenges? Are such questions freezing life in a place where we are merely attempting to cope and survive?"

SACRED PURPOSE

In the world today, we often see people struggling, unhappy, depressed, alienated, frustrated, or appearing lost and in a day-to-day battle to survive. As a result, we have seen an increase in a wide variety of symptoms of imbalance, which include: sleep disorders, relationship difficulties, family disconnection, back and neck pain, headaches, weight issues, gastrointestinal issues, diabetes, fibromyalgia, chronic illness, dysfunctional and antisocial behaviors manifesting in violence, criminal activity, substance abuse, nihilism, and oppressed motivation, in an attempt to survive day to day. In addition, for many, poverty, racism, sexism, misogyny, discrimination, inequality, and injustice has created or at least contributed to these issues and certainly inhibit personal development, making it difficult to improve our circumstances. On a personal, familial, and communal level, many of these issues are merely symptoms of not being in balance, feeling devalued, unaccepted, or not worthy; in essence, being disconnected from our true sacredness and sacred purpose.

So, we travel down this road in search of ways to face the issues that cause us discomfort and dis-ease; in search of teachings that can guide us to reconnect with our true meaning in life and find our balance. The deeper question for some is, "How do I find balance and meaning in spite of my issues?"

In the indigenous language of my ancestors, the state of being connected to one's sacred self and sacred purpose is called *In Tloque Nahuaque*, or the interconnection to all that is near and far that is sacred. In other words, being one with God. Part of this search for interconnected sacredness is the ultimate hope that the cycles of trauma, sometimes several generations deep, will be healed. The pain of the negative forces of addiction, shame and fear will be lessened so that the next generation will carry more blessings and sacred teachings, and less burdens of self-destruction and disconnection.

I believe that's why my grandmother and many elders loved to work in her garden because when life challenges you and you distrust the world, nature is always there. She was connecting to the sacredness and constancy of nature, which often times is the only thing you can count on. For traditional people, connecting to nature and the sacred elements was/is vital and essential to daily life. This was one of the ways my grandmother maintained her sacred connection. And although I was raised in Compton, California, which was and is considered a pretty tough place to live, I remember hearing my grandmother early in the morning begin every day with prayer. It was her *connecting practice*, after which she would go to her garden to water and talk to the plants. Throughout the day, we would find her sitting in her chair with her eyes closed. We thought she was asleep, but if we said anything that pertained to her or we weren't behaving, she would respond immediately. In a similar way, when I would go over to pick up my best friend,

Tyrone, from school, I would see his grandmother, Gramma Moseley, in prayerful reflection on the front porch of her house. I thought she too was asleep, but I now recognize that these grandmothers were not asleep at all. They were in a state of deep reflection, also referred to by some traditions as meditation. What I didn't realize at the time was that they were praying for me, and all our family, and that their relationship with the plants was also their way of staying in balance with creation. So even in Compton, these elders incorporated their own sacred rituals for self-care, in their daily lives. In different cultures and spiritual paths, this practice of sacred connection is also found in sweat lodge ceremonies, churches, synagogues, temples, *danza*, art or poetry.

Regardless of the practice or what it is called, all of these traditions provide a way to reinforce one's connection and purpose to a higher power. That sacredness includes all our relations, including our connection to the plants and animals, water and air, sun and moon, and all things in the universe, especially the children. In fact, it is the belief of indigenous people that children come into this world from the Creator and Ancestors as sacred beings, with their purpose intact. They come into this world for a divine reason that will add and contribute to the world in a positive way.

It doesn't matter how the child arrived here, whether in a relationship where the parents planned for the birth, or if the child came into this world in difficult circumstances where the parents were not ready to receive, care for, or even love the child. According to ancient teachings, all children, regardless of the circumstances of their birth, are sacred and have a sacred purpose, and all people should be acknowledged and embraced that way.

In line with that thinking, I remember recently leading a blessing ceremony for twin infant girls, daughters of very close friends of mine. And as I was doing the ceremony, I began to share with those present that when these children were born, they were sacred. They came from the sacred source; they came from God, the Creator. They came into this world in a sacred way, a blessed way. They came with their sacred purpose already present within their spirit. That is why babies have such pure responses to life. They cry without hesitation when they are hungry or have a dirty diaper. They will laugh when someone makes a funny face. They will kick or jump if they are startled. They sleep when they are tired; and when they are not, they will not, regardless of routine. They effortlessly respond to the inherent sacred rhythm within them.

During the blessing ceremony, I shared that the importance of this tradition was to offer unconditional *acknowledgement and acceptance* for these two little girls - welcoming them into the world just the way they are, with their inherent sacredness and purpose. The true meaning of the gathering was to welcome these children and for all present to make a commitment to support these little girls in *remembering their sacredness* and *cultivating their sacred purpose* throughout their lives. While these babies were born sacred, it was incumbent upon their parents and circle of relations to remind them of their sacredness, help them manifest it, and live accordingly; because life can at times be cruel and often reinforces the opposite message, especially for children of certain populations.

But many of us may not have come into the world acknowledged as a blessing, or welcomed in such a way, or even been given the message that we were *wanted*. For this reason, all indigenous cultures across the world have a ceremony or tradition for *welcoming and acknowledging* others, recognizing that this is the first teaching in life. The communal act of acknowledging and accepting the new life as part of their relations, making it very clear that a child is *wanted*, and a valued part of the community, is seen as fundamental and essential to a child's well-being. Although the practice or tradition of *acknowledgement and welcoming* may seem like common sense, we recognize that many of these traditional ways have been invalidated or lost, due to a variety of reasons. In addition, sometimes our own parents have been shamed and ridiculed for attempting to practice these traditions so have abandoned them along the way. In addition, other members of our families may have unresolved wounds which make it difficult enough just to survive, let alone extend themselves in love and acknowledgement, even to their own children.

Nevertheless, when this acknowledgement, welcoming and connection message does not get fulfilled, one can carry the emptiness and woundedness throughout their entire life, searching for validation from anyone willing to give it to them. For this reason, various cultures would collectively take on the responsibility of facilitating welcoming as the root of positive identity and belonging.

In my own experience and in reference to this welcoming tradition, I remember when I was a little boy, when someone in our family had a baby we would always go visit the baby and take some food.[3] In preparation for our first visit, we were told that upon meeting the baby, we must touch the

---

[3] Food for our culture was an offering of gratitude, and making a commitment to assist in *nourishing* the child.

baby and say something beautiful about the child. I didn't understand why we needed to touch the child and was given an explanation that if you didn't, the baby might get sick (Mal de ojo).[4] Later in studying the basis of the tradition, I discovered that the true purpose of touching the baby was to welcome the child and to acknowledge the *connection* we had to the child. The tradition of touching or saying something positive acknowledged the energy. Words, looks, or anything else directed at the child impressed the feeling of a blessing. Conversely, it also brings to light the tremendous effect that a harmful or negative act, look or feeling can have on someone's life, especially as a child.

We see manifestations of this when someone is treated in a negative way, and then processes this as feeling unwanted, or perceives that he does not meet the expectations of his family, community, or society. The experience can definitely impact a child, or adult, in a painful way throughout life. I've witnessed many adults who are very accomplished and recipients of many accolades, but still long for the acknowledgment of their father or the love of their mother. It also points to the societal and generational impact that racism, sexism, homophobia, xenophobia or other judgement-based oppression can have on an individual, family or culture of people, when they carry deep-seated insecurity or shame from how society views or treats them. The feeling early on of being unworthy, unloved, or not meeting the expectations among basic circles of relations, can affect a person's self-worth, self-

---

[4]In traditional Mexican culture it is believed that if you only admire a baby by looking at them and don't touch them(connection) then the baby may get sick.

image, and long-term sense of sacredness and sacred purpose.

With this in mind, it is no wonder why it is sometimes difficult for many of us to have good relations, or be able to trust and connect with others in an intimate way. By reflecting on this teaching, and recognizing the power of acknowledgement and acceptance, it may give us insight into one source of our woundedness and the need for healing. It is important to remember that the *sacredness* and the *sacred purpose* that I write of was present when your life began and still lives deep within your spirit. The questions now become: "If we are not connected to our sacredness or are unsure how to retrieve it, can it be recovered? And if so, how do we go about doing that? How can we discover our true selves again? How can we uncover our very essence so that we can, once again, be in alignment with the Creator and the ancestors - our *sacred purpose*, *In Tloque Nahuaque*, interconnected sacredness and our connection to God?"

Obviously this is easier said than done, especially in a society that does not lend itself toward validating or respecting the indigenous worldview of life. We live in a society which reinforces the idea that babies come into this world as blank slates. Others believe that babies are born with sin or negativity within them. And the dominant culture reinforces that institutions must *teach you* who you are and by acquiring knowledge in these institutions, you will become a *valued* part of society. Now let me be very clear, I believe there is valuable knowledge and skills that the educational institutions can offer people in terms of obtaining a job and preparing for a career. In this respect, getting a formal education is very important. However, formal education as presently structured does not provide a path to overall human development which will enable a person to deal with challenges posed by a modern society. In fact, today's dominant culture and societal norms reinforce patterns and habits that often pull people away from their relationships and sacred purpose. These norms often encourage habits and practices that are more materialistic and less focused on true happiness and harmony in life. Nevertheless, in spite of these barriers, there are people who live in a sacred way, and have incorporated practices that keep them connected and balanced. The practice of maintaining this way of life is difficult, but not impossible. So let us explore the teachings and practices that can enable us to move in this direction and uncover, recover and discover our *sacredness* and our sacred purpose once again.

CHAPTER 3
ACKNOWLEDGING YOUR SACREDNESS

"Some people come into your life as blessings, some come into your life as lessons."

-MOTHER TERESA

I have the blessing of being connected with Huichol elders, who are traditional indigenous people that come from the High Sierras of Mexico. They visit us yearly at the Sacred Circles Center where we do some of this work. These elders came for a few days to administer blessings and healings, and to counsel people. Many people came to the Center to receive this medicine. During a break, I asked one of the elders if he wanted something to drink. He asked for some coffee, so I served him some and served myself a cup as well. The elder wanted some sugar and milk, so I added them to the cup and gave it to him, and left the spoon in the cup. Watching him with a simple cup of coffee, I learned a powerful lesson. Drinking a cup of coffee or tea is something many of us do every day. We make or buy a cup of coffee, we put sugar and cream in it, and mix it up without much thought, so we can get to drinking it. But what I saw when I gave this elder the coffee was something very different. I saw him dip the spoon down into the coffee, and ladle it up; dip it down, and ladle it up again and again, maybe about twenty times. By the time he had finished stirring his coffee, I had already gulped mine down, probably not even tasting it. As he continued his ladling ritual, he was looking in the cup and watching, almost like he was watching a river flow or following the rhythmic waves of the ocean. The elder remained completely focused and concentrated on his coffee. After he finished, he got the cup, brought it to his nose and inhaled it deeply, obviously enjoying the aroma. Only then did he finally take a sip of it, closing his eyes as if it was nectar. It was as if I could see the sip of coffee go down and through him with a sense of joy.

SHOWING UP AND BEING PRESENT

There he sat drinking his coffee. It was such a wonderful dance to witness, such a beautifully authentic teaching of how one can stay connected to the sacredness of a moment in life. What I had experienced in watching this Huichol elder, was a practical demonstration of the first lesson: Maintaining our sacredness. In essence, the act of *showing up and being present* is a manifestation of feeling worthy enough to honor the sacred moment, and to show up and be in joy where you are at. It seems like such a simple thing to do. But what does showing up and being present really mean? I'm sure you've heard people say "live for the moment". Well, there is more to it than that. It means, that in order to be able to maintain our sacredness, we must first *acknowledge and accept* ourselves by showing up and being present for day to day things including the lessons and blessings that life presents. The problem is that we may try to show up and enjoy life, but society also complicates things by reinforcing the opposite. For example, by promoting instant gratification, hyper-dependence on technology, or praising multi-tasking as a virtue. At the same time, some of us may not realize that we are stuck in a pattern (lesson) of attempting to ignore the wounds by keeping busy, which is another way to avoid being present.

Unfortunately, some of us are so used to simply surviving or getting by in existence mode, that we don't even know the difference. We don't realize how much of the time we are robotically moving through life, just doing, rather than being. In fact, we often overwhelm ourselves with so much to do, that we don't even create time and space to just *be*. What we also don't realize, is that one of the residual symptoms of unresolved pain (i.e. not being fully welcomed, acknowledged or accepted; being rejected or abused) manifests in the *inability* to be present. Whether it be in our bodies, in our relationships, or to be fully present in other meaningful aspects of our lives or with simple things like enjoying a cup of coffee. Some of us get *stuck* in the pain and trauma of the past and live life reacting to situations based on our wounded selves - as if it is normal to move through life busily and detached.

My ancestors would call this place, *Susto*, or being stuck in a trauma-based state. This state of disconnection makes it difficult for many of us to truly enjoy life or stay focused in our present relationships. It promotes a way of life that is based on unconsciously avoiding feeling; therefore, not truly being able to enjoy the life we have. As time goes on with each passing day, just like a drug, it takes more and more stimulation, excitement, and material goods to sedate the anxiety of this disconnection. These patterns of behavior can even be passed on from generation to generation becoming what I call *relational tribal patterns*. If you were raised with these patterns, you may unknowingly think this is just the normal way of life. In reference to patterns and behaviors, I've heard people say, "Oh my family is just crazy, we always sarcastically joke and tease one another." In actuality, they are putting each other down to maintain distance. Others demonstrate dramatic patterns, or routinely fight and make up, accepting this process as normal and dividing themselves based on dysfunction: the side each individual is on is determined by whether you go along with these patterns of mutual dysfunction or behavior patterns. If one goes along, she/he belongs. If one questions or challenges these destructive ways, she/he is ostracized or rejected or many times accused of "thinking you're better than us."

On the other hand, what I saw in the Huichol elder drinking his coffee, was this ability to truly enjoy even the most simple of things. He was fully present, en-joying (in joy) the beauty of his experience, nothing else distracting him. If we can't even do that with a cup of coffee, then it will be more difficult for us to do this in relationships. Unfortunately, our society rewards people for doing the opposite; for multi-tasking or not staying focused on one thing. We even give praise and awards to those who have mastered this, those who appear to be effectively doing several things at once. This multi-tasking mentality is so pervasive in our society that we even have to pass laws to forbid texting and driving at the same time, or putting on makeup and driving.

How can we truly drive and text at the same time? Or put makeup on while driving safely? The reality is that you truly can't do more than one thing at a time. You may attempt to text and drive, but at any given moment you are really only doing one thing, however distracted as your mind works to keep track of the other. Dividing attention is mentally draining and depleting, and the quality with which the distinct actions are done is ultimately sacrificed. The end result is getting further and further estranged from the joy or the essence of whatever we're doing. You may have experienced eating a bag of chips or cookies, while you are watching TV. All of the sudden, the potato chips or cookies are gone. And then you say to yourself, "Man, who ate all those potato chips?" Well, you ate them. But you didn't enjoy them and probably didn't really taste or digest them properly. It was just something that you were doing as you were watching TV. The problem is that eating is supposed to be a self-nurturing act, which is impossible if we're not really present.

The reality is we can't truly nurture ourselves (eat) if we are distracted. We then wonder why so many of us are overweight, or have digestive problems. Our food has trouble digesting because we aren't present as we are digesting the food. All of the senses need to be engaged to digest our food properly, and instead we are sending the body and mind mixed signals. With that said, I will acknowledge that in certain circumstances, it is necessary to "multitask." In certain jobs or even parenting our children, at times it is important. However, the problem arises when this becomes habitual and spills into our everyday relationships. What happens when one is never really present in who he is and what he is doing? The end result is that we become robotic.

DOING THINGS MAÑANA (TOMORROW)

As a youngster, I remember asking my mom if we could do something and she would say *"mañana mijo,"* which means, "tomorrow my son." In retrospect, I thought such exchanges were just an old fashioned Mexican way of my mother dismissing or just putting me off. What I didn't realize at the time is that my mother was focused on that task at hand and didn't want to be distracted from what she was doing. When we are always thinking about something else, the next place we need to be, or what's coming tomorrow, it takes energy away from what is presently being done. By continuing to do things this way, we end up with a less-than-satisfactory experience. As our minds get trained to not fully enjoy the present, where we are and what we are doing, we end up always wanting more, or being discontent with what we have. This may lead to a perpetual feeling of dissatisfaction in our lives. We all know people who continually complain and never seem to be satisfied. They are always envious or jealous of others; they want to be someplace else, with someone else, or have what someone else has.

This behavior can become a long-term pattern, and affect one's relationships. A sense of distraction or dissatisfaction is one of the most destructive things that I see that occurs with couples that I counsel; especially when one of the partners no longer wants to be in the relationship. The question then becomes whether he is unhappy with his partner, or just unhappy with his own life. Many times the person doesn't even know.

Even more devastating is when it becomes obvious years later that one partner truly never loved or committed to his spouse in the first place. This typically means that the discontented person never really showed up to fully commit himself to his partner. Too often the results are infidelity or unfaithfulness as a consequence of that missing connection, lack of commitment or inability to fully show up. Imagine being married to someone for 10, 20, or 30 years and then realizing that person never really committed to you wholeheartedly. He never said, "I'm going to be present with you; not with anyone else, just with you."

"In the midst of turmoil and chaos,

keep stillness inside of you."

-DEEPAK CHOPRA

It is something that I hear quite often in my counseling practice from people, especially women, that their partner doesn't ever listen to them. The descriptions are disturbingly similar, "You know, he's not listening. He hears, but he's not listening. It seems like he's not even here. He's not present. He's always watching television or talking on the phone, texting or playing video games." And in reference to sexuality and intimacy, we see many couples report that, even though they are having sex, it seems like her/his partner is not there. They report such things as: "He can't even look me in the eye. He won't even kiss me passionately. It seems like he just wants to get off. He's there, but not really there. He's thinking about something else." It works both ways, though, and some of the descriptions I've heard from males have included, "She's thinking about something or someone else. While having sex she is thinking about the laundry she didn't finish."

So this inability to be present can spill over in everything we do. Even more alarming is when one partner brings it up, and the other is totally oblivious to the disconnection. For that person, the disconnection or lack of intimacy has become the norm.

To further contribute to this common state of absence, the role of mass media, computer technology, and the internet have added an additional dimension to the personal disconnection. In today's society, computers, cell phones, Wi-Fi and diverse modalities of boundless streaming are wonderful and have added so much to our global interaction. Conversely, the social norm has moved us to a place where we're not even present when we are interacting. Alone or in the company of others, we are texting, we're emailing, we're skyping, and we never turn off energetically, causing confusion in our mind, body and spirit. We're able to fly from one part of the country to the other in a matter of hours. In the end, our bodies may have gone from Los Angeles to New York, but our spirits take longer to get there. Energetically this is very confusing. Physiologically, this disconnection can mess with the natural rhythms of our bodies, minds and spirits, and throw us way off balance. Therefore, it is important for us to make a commitment to work on acknowledging ourselves by being present in our lives and relationships.

"What are you reacting to? Ask

Yourself that question every moment of

everyday when your peace is

disturbed. "

-KENNETH WAPNICK

MEDICATING OUR DISCONNECTION

So how do we deal with disconnection? As a society, we have come to approach the symptoms of disconnection and the inability to be present, in a very strange way. Oftentimes, when someone is hurt, sick, depressed or just feeling sad, we right away want to medicate him, ostensibly, to make them feel better or take away the symptoms. We want to get him out of his present state of feeling, without really exploring what brought on that feeling, imbalance or discomfort in the first place. We immediately try to take that person out of being present with his sadness or anxiety. What we don't understand is that the body, heart, mind, and spirit are magnificent teachers. Sometimes, a person needs to feel down in order to slow down and allow oneself to reflect, learn a lesson, and rebalance.

It's not bad to be down, slow down, be contemplative, or go inside; even though some people might label that as being *depressed.* Often, these feelings or behavioral responses are interpreted as being weak or crazy. On the other hand, there is much value and strength in being able to *slow down*, to connect with mother earth and learn from one's experience.

Sometimes, slowing us down is the only way that the Creator can get our attention, and in doing so, gives us a whole new view of our situation or circumstance. It stops or slows us to a pace that allows us time to reflect. However, society's reactive pattern of encouraging us to not be present, or understand where we are and what circumstances mean in relation to our purpose, is unhealthy. Worse yet, this reinforces what society is telling us about how we *shouldn't feel or shouldn't be, and* how we *need to change*. The process also reinforces the practice of sedating the present feeling - e.g. have a beer, smoke a joint, or take some medication in order to not feel this any longer. This also carries over to how we deal with our children, where instead of trying to understand a child or a teen's restlessness or their anger, we want to sedate him, buy her a new video game or send him to an anger management class.

This pressure to sedate or to mask rather than cure our woundedness is another way society moves us away from learning the teaching *of honoring our sacredness and thus, being present.* Often, this societal pressure and critically judgmental point of view doesn't allow us to really experience the teachings or the lessons that await us. It is no wonder why many of us find ourselves stuck in dysfunctional patterns or behaviors for a lifetime, because we never truly addressed the underlying cause of the imbalance.

So, as we begin to think about shifting these patterns, especially as it pertains to our relationships, the first person we need to learn to have a positive relationship with is ourself. Yes, the first step to acknowledging our sacredness and being present is *being able to acknowledge, accept, and be present with ourselves*. We begin this by acknowledging and accepting who we are, right here and now.

The *you* that is present today. Not the person that you used to be or want to be, but the one that you are right now with both the blessings and the challenges. Only then can you begin having a sacred relationship with yourself; not who people have said you are, or their expectation of whom they want you to be, but loving and being present with your true sacred self as you are today. Accepting who you are now is the first step. This doesn't mean that there are not things that you could do better or change, but you must first accept the truth of who you are right now.

CONNECTING WITH YOUR PRESENT SACREDNESS

Another part of rediscovering our sacredness is undoing messages or patterns that stifle our authentic selves. Growing up, many of us have been told how we should or shouldn't be. We were told not to do this or we can't be like that. For instance, being told we can't cry, not to laugh too loud, or not to be too wild. In addition, many people of color or oppressed populations have been made to feel ashamed of who they are because of their race, color of their skin, gender identity, or patterns of behavior that didn't fit the *norm*. This negative reinforcement creates fear of being one's true self. Some of us were taught regimented ways of being, based on the dominant society's norms - compounded by one's own cultural and family's expectations.

Growing up, I remember hearing countless rules and criticisms. This was especially so for my sisters. They were told, "You have to be respectful. You can't be too loud or too expressive. Make sure you sit with your legs closed and wear a long dress." If one didn't do this, she was judged or ridiculed. In this way, girls many times are made to feel inadequate and constantly judged, which doesn't really allow them to be who they truly are. They are taught what *not* to do or how *not* to behave, sometimes based on a parent's or family member's fears or old wounds. In such an environment, their spirit becomes trapped. We need to realize the damage these kinds of conditional, negative oriented demands place on one's spirit. On the other hand, little boys are also given messages. They are told, "Don't cry. Don't be a sissy. Suck up the pain. What is the matter with you? Are you weak?" It is this kind of reactive messaging that teaches a person not to feel, which has resulted in many men today not able to be present with their emotions, or having difficulty staying focused and being present in an intimate relationship.

Inevitably, these messages begin to move us, *through fear*, away from who we really are as sacred people. The result is major confusion in the person's sense of self, and a disconnection from their sacred being. Where there is no acknowledgment of one's sense of sacredness, there is little room for feelings of spontaneity, joy, and being present in one's life. Without this acknowledgment, our sacredness gets lost or frozen (Susto).

If this confusion starts in childhood, it can continue into adolescence and create issues with learning, retaining, and task completion. This can lead to picking up counter-productive, addictive patterns to try to compensate. By adolescence though, many teenagers have developed the will to say what they feel or what they want. As a response to the early denial of their true self, they often "overreact." A teenager might say what they want, do whatever they want, or act any way they please, regardless of the consequences. Although this may be an understandable reaction by teens, society may see this as dysfunctional, or as bad behavior, acting crazy, and being disrespectful. In reaction to this, society labels these young people as rebellious, belligerent, or anti-social. These teens may comb their hair the way they want, wearing it straight up in the air with all kinds of product, dressing in what might be considered outlandish clothes, and listening to what some would deem crazy music. What is really going on is that they're actually listening to their spirit and attempting to call it back from all the rules, criticisms, and judgments, while at the same time reacting to the confusing and inconsistent messages they see and receive from the adults and society in general.

Additionally, if they have grown up in a home where they have been abused physically, emotionally, mentally or sexually, it is difficult to want, or feel safe enough, to be present in their body, mind and emotions. This is especially true when one's existence is filled with criticism and judgment. What one's spirit hears and interprets from all of these actions is, "I'm not valued, seen or heard at all, so there must be something wrong with me." This can then lead to more intrusive thoughts or feelings that maybe they are a mistake, not supposed to be here, unwanted, or that the world would be better off without them. The prevalence of messages inferred in this way can reverberate in a young person's, or person of any age's, head and lead to other, more serious issues.

Those who have grown up in these circumstances can even begin to believe that they are cursed, that something is wrong with them, or that they're the bad seed/black sheep of the family. When reinforced by critical adults, some people believe that when they are present, bad things happen. When your spirit becomes damaged to this extent, *you do not even realize that you are sacred anymore* or that you have a sacred purpose at all. When a person gets used to those messages, they may unconsciously seek out people who reinforce the same negative, critical feelings. Worse yet, they may end up feeling that they deserve the negative comments, negative feelings, and the negative treatment. When people get to that vulnerable place, they often end up not knowing who they truly are anymore. They end up living based on their wounded selves rather than their sacred selves. They may even feel like they are outside of their bodies, not knowing how they should be, who they should be, or if they should *be*, at all.

When a person gets to such a desperate place, there's an overwhelming feeling of hopelessness, pessimism, and deep depression that sometimes leads to wanting to hurt one's self or worse. On the road to this negative habitual place, is where people pick up self-destructive ways to not feel, or to simply cope. They may use drugs and/or alcohol, sabotage positive opportunities in their lives, and even do things that destroy their relationships. They'll hurt themselves physically and may end up hurting others. Or they'll become promiscuous, giving their bodies and sacredness to other people without any thought.

On the other end of the spectrum, even though it may seem unrelated, there are those people that attempt to shut down the same, ugly feelings of disconnection within themselves by rescuing others. They become the rescuers, the perfectionists, the workaholics, and the do-gooders. And many times they attempt to rescue and save those that sabotage themselves. Unfortunately, it is never enough. They can never do enough or work enough, because in doing so much with such high expectations, they too are attempting to sedate their own true feelings. By focusing on others or in a litany of tasks, they are distracted from accepting and acknowledging who they really are, or their own limitations. In the end, they end up exhausted, depressed, frustrated and hopeless; just as lost as those that they are trying to rescue. In essence, two people functioning on the opposite ends of the same negative energetic track.

For those of us in this state of imbalance, it may seem like such a long journey back. Many times we don't even know what true balance, harmony, or sacredness feels like anymore. It seems impossible to be able to recover, discover, or uncover a sacredness that we can't even remember. What we don't realize is that in spite of all these burdens and obstacles, sacredness still exists in the essence of our spirits and is only one breath away.

"Sometimes unforeseen opportunities emerge from the remnants of life's challenges. Sometimes it is possible to transform tough times into great growth and success."

-KAY DOUGLAS

CHAPTER 4

WAKE UP AND SAY, "GOOD MORNING," TO YOURSELF

"O' GREAT SPIRIT... help me always to speak the truth quietly, to listen with an open mind when others speak, and to remember the peace that may be found in silence."

-CHEROKEE PRAYER

Although we may feel hopeless at times, our sacredness never leaves us. It's just that life can move us to disconnect from that sacredness and we forget who we truly are. Fortunately, our Sacredness and our Sacred Purpose can be recovered with the very simple step of choosing to be present in our lives again. This begins with the profound acknowledgement of who we truly are. We need to recognize that the Creator, God, the Great Universe, or whatever higher power you connect with, doesn't create junk. And even though you may have made mistakes along your journey in life, YOU are *NOT a mistake*. Even though your patterns and behaviors may seem unhealthy and even hurtful to yourself or others, your behaviors don't change the essence of who you are. Everyone that comes into this world is a blessing. *I am sacred and a blessing just the way I am.* The question then becomes, "How do we bring the essence of our sacredness into the physical, emotional, mental and spiritual aspects of our lives, and then live them?" So, let's begin to put into practice a sacred process of honoring and recovering our true selves.

All people in their indigenous practices, traditions or ceremonies, have rituals of connecting to nature to reinforce the energy of sacredness. Through their prayer, chants, songs or mantras, they reconnect with the ancestral energies. Unfortunately, not all of us have had access to, or knowledge of these ancestral ways. And others have disconnected from these ways or have been taught that they were not significant. The teaching of *In Tloque Nahuaque,* or being connected to one's sacredness, begins simply with you choosing to create a sacred space and time for yourself. The act of creating space and time is not much different than what my grandmother would do every morning when she would begin her day in prayer. She would go to her altar, light her candles and begin her sacred prayer. So, let us move into that space.

IN TLOQUE
NAHUAQUE
Interconnected
Sacredness

Sacred Life Teachings

Some of us attempting this process for the first time may wonder how it is going to help, especially if there is no belief in one's own sacredness or sacred purpose. But it's similar to questioning how the grass or trees can be sacred when they have yellow spots and seem to be unhealthy or dormant from growth. The saying goes, "The grass is greener on the other side." The truth is the grass is greener where it is *watered and nourished.* So, the questions become, "What do you want to water? What do you want to grow, and what are you willing to feed?" In reality, the energetic, affirmative vibration of what you put out and how you live will manifest and grow. So, it is important, every morning, to intentionally *wake up and say, "Good morning," to your sacred self.*

The next questions then become, "How do I embrace and integrate this message into who I am? How do I maintain the transformation and growth?" It may be awkward at first, and it may even seem phony, but it starts with that very first step of choosing to be present in your life; to show up as whoever you are, and to embrace your sacredness. Whether you're 15, 35, or even 75, the first decision that you must commit to is being intentional and consistent in the journey back to your sacredness. It starts with you choosing to show up for you, at your present place in life, with all your light and darkness. Stand straight up, or kneel down, and face your truth. You may be there with many wounds, but life is about night and day. It's about darkness and light. It's about facing that duality and accepting our present state of growth in awareness... but it must be without judgment. Judgment is what has gotten many of us stuck in the first place; first, alienated from others, and then from ourselves.

That's why Grandfather Sun comes up every morning - to remind us that we have that light within us, that every day the light is there. We just have to show up like Grandfather Sun does every day - without the masks, without the shame, without excuses, without sedating, and welcome our self to a new day of learning, growing, healing and living.

"I love that this morning's sunrise does

not define itself by last night's sunset."

-DR. STEVE MARABOLI

The journey then becomes searching for that light within us. We have to wake up and say good morning to our authentic selves. Not the person others have told you that you are, but to your sacred self. Not the one we are thinking we want to be, but the one connected to the sacredness of God, the Creator, and the universe, right now, today. We have to be present with ourselves and acknowledge that wherever we are in our lives today, is where we are supposed to be, sacred as we are.

This foundation will then allow you to recognize that just because you may have some habits, behaviors, and ways that need to change, that transformation begins by you showing up and embracing your total self, beginning with the light. In no way does this justify someone's hurtful or self-destructive behaviors, but you must recognize that in order to correct counterproductive patterns, a person must first embrace their sacred selves and then be ready to face the darkness within. We can't be afraid or ashamed of going into that night, which is a part of us as well, to acknowledge and face the true wholeness of who we are.

"No hay mal que por bien no venga"

(Even when something seemingly bad

happens, goodness can come from it.)

-MEXICAN PROVERB

If you're afraid to go into the night, you'll never see the stars; you'll never experience the quietness and the peacefulness of that nighttime glow. In fact, we find that many wonderful healers, teachers, and therapists have received their medicine through their own experience with their darkness. In essence, by going through some very horrible experiences, coming to terms with them, and finding the lessons, they now have medicine to help others. Although originating in the darkness, the medicine becomes light, part of their whole, true, sacred purpose.

Being present and showing up in your life, acknowledging who you are and accepting who you are, is the first step. It's about accepting who you are with a sense of blessing and thanksgiving, and recognizing that everything that you've experienced up to this point, can serve you. Everything that has happened in your life up until now makes you *who* you really are. And within that *who*, resides the sacredness. The sacredness is waiting for you to show up, to be there, and to appreciate the essence of who you are. It can begin with just one deep breath, just a sense of being where you are right now, just appreciating the present, giving thanks that you have this moment.

Many ancient healers and teachers teach the importance of beginning with a prayer or meditation. This is called *centering*. Whatever it means within your culture or world-view, the intention is to be *In Tloque Nahuaque*, as one with God and the universe. The blessings that are given to us through our breath, the wind spirit, our essence of being, through our sense of consciousness, connects us to our sacred selves. This in turn opens a channel for grace and healing. As we begin to incorporate this life view through practice, we may also begin to recollect other times of grace experienced in our lives.

If we really take the time think about it, we can all identify such moments in our lives. Perhaps it was witnessing a baby being born, or a child doing something very precious, a moment where certain music touched us so deeply that we cried, or we recognized the natural wonder of a beautiful waterfall. The experience may have taken place during a special moment in a church service or spiritual ceremony, and is an instance where we feels God's presence, the spirit of life, or energy shared by all living things. It is in those moments that we are connected to the sacredness within us. All we had to do was show up for the experience and allow the blessing to come through us. It seems like such a simple step, possibly even too simple to really make a difference, especially if we are in a deep place of darkness, depression or pain. What I am asking you to do is believe that the teachings work. While the steps or process I have described may appear simple, putting these lessons into practice can be very difficult for those who have not been able to connect to their sacredness in a long while, or ever.

> *"Meditation is not meant to help us avoid problems or run away from difficulties. It is meant to allow positive healing to take place. To meditate is to learn how to stop - to stop being carried away by our regrets about the past, our anger or despair in the present, or our worries about the future."*
>
> *-THICH NHAT HANH*

MAKING A COMMITMENT TO YOUR SACREDNESS

Living in your sacredness is a very important commitment. Developing a practice for watering the sacred within you is based on your willingness to consider that regardless of what has happened in your life, you can still be grateful for where you are right now. To set the foundation, we will begin with a prayer of acknowledgement, of *"I am Sacred, I am a Blessing."* I ask you to commit to starting with the first step of showing up, being present, and making a choice to practice those things that assist you in becoming the true essence of who you really are. Here are some suggestions on how to begin your practice of honoring yourself.

I would recommend that you *create a special space, altar,* or spot where you go every day to ground yourself.

On this altar, you can place special objects, sacred elements, herbs and/or pictures of ancestors and loved ones. As you continue to pray, your altar will gain energy and spirit. In many traditions, people incorporate the use of herbs (sage, copal, tobacco, and/or incense) and sounds (flute, drums, nature sounds) to further engage their senses, connect with their genetic sound vibrations of ancestors, and bring themselves into focus with their present state of consciousness.

Choose to spend a few minutes each day, twice a day if possible, feeling, breathing, getting connected to the Creator, acknowledging your sacredness and giving thanks for who you are. Choose to devote just 5 minutes in the morning and 5 minutes before you go to sleep, to this journey of honoring and healing yourself. The reality is: if you cannot devote just 10 minutes a day to yourself, then you are not ready to move in this direction. Just try it for 28 days (1 moon cycle) to begin with.

It may be helpful to record these instructions and then play them back to guide you through the process until you have integrated the process.

- Let's begin the morning ritual by connecting with the earth around you, by honoring and feeling the ground and connecting your energy to the earth. Connect to the sounds in your present environment; listen, feel, sense the sacred moment.

- Stop in the quiet of the moment, close your eyes and take a minute to open yourself to healing and blessings.

- Then connect with the sacredness of the moment by taking a slow deep breath in through your nose all the way to the pit of your stomach and then slowly exhaling out through your mouth. Take 3 more breaths in and out in the same way as you honor the moment.

- Now say, **"I am sacred, I am a blessing."**

- Inhale, then exhale. Now say it again, **"I am sacred, I am a blessing."** Hear it. Inhale, then exhale.

- Now imagine that your ancestors, your grandmothers, are saying it to you. Say it again **"I am sacred, I am a blessing."** Hear, feel, and take in their message. Do this 4 times, each time inhaling and exhaling slowly.

- Now sit with this thought and feeling for a minute. And if you need to repeat the process, you can do it again - each time sitting with it for a while.

- Attempt to carry this sacredness throughout the day. Show up and be present in your own life, for your own well-being.

- Show up and be present in the lives of your relationships.

The next part of this sacred ritual is the practice you do **at night, before you go to sleep**. It is focused on being grateful for your connection to the universe.

- Begin by connecting with the earth around you, by honoring and feeling the ground and connecting your energy to where you are. Connect to the sounds in your present environment. Listen, feel, sense the sacred moment.

- Then close your eyes and connect with the sacredness of the moment by taking a deep breath in through your nose, and slowly out through your mouth.

- Stop in the quiet of the moment, and take a minute to open yourself to healing and blessings.

- Take a deep breath in, and then exhale slowly. Connect with your breath and your body again. Inhale, then exhale.

- Hear yourself say it, feel it and embrace it. Inhale, then exhale.

- Now give thanks for whomever and wherever you are right now, without criticism and without judgement (criticism and judgment take you out of your sacredness).

- Now say, **"I want to thank you, Creator, for who I am and the lessons in my life."** Say it 4 times, inhaling and exhaling in between each.

- Give thanks, recognizing that wherever you are right now, is where you are supposed to be.

- Recall all the things you feel grateful for today.

- Be with that sense of your sacredness.

- Now say, "**I put all of my burdens and worries in your hands, as I honor myself by allowing my body to rest.**" Inhale and release. Say this 4 times.

- Attempt to carry this sacredness with you, as you allow yourself to rest through the night.

- Try committing to do this practice for one moon cycle (around 28 days). Just 5 minutes in the morning and 5 minutes in the evening. You will see how it begins a process of recovering your sacredness.

Now that you are on your journey again, the ancestors, elders, angels, Creator and all of the universe will walk with you as you choose to incorporate the first teaching of In *Tloque Nahuaque: acknowledging* your sacredness and recovering your Sacred Purpose into your life.

"Nothing is more powerful than a

surrendered life in the hands of God."

-RICK WARREN

CHAPTER 5

PAY ATTENTION: THE ANCESTORS ARE READY TO EMBRACE YOU

"People are sent into our lives to teach us things that we need to learn about ourselves."

-MANDY HALE

As you now have begun to incorporate the practice of In Tloque Nahuaque, or acknowledging your sacredness by being present, you are prepared to begin incorporating the second lesson- the lesson of In Lak'ech, or paying attention to life as your *reflective* teacher. This Mayan teaching of In Lak'ech (you are my other me) is the concept that everything in life is a reflective teaching (your other you).

IN TLOQUE
NAHUAQUE
Interconnected
Sacredness

IN LAK'ECH
You Are My Other Me

Sacred Life Teachings

Within this teaching, the elders would describe this lesson as life's mirror, *el espejo*, or the way that life and all its experiences reflect teachings to us. This is as opposed to thinking that things just happen to us or that are a victims of circumstances. This seems like a small difference but this shift can change our entire perspective. Unfortunately, we often miss the significance of life or our relationships as teachers because modern society tends to make us think that the important teachings are only learned in an institution, by science, or taught to us by credentialed people or licensed therapists. It also categorizes life's experiences as good or bad, positive or negative, with a focus on labeling certain experiences as even pathological. It uses this *judgment* as a way of labeling these experiences with an emotional weight, often making us feel inadequate, ashamed, or irreparably damaged if we've experienced certain things. This labeling or categorization then tends to create *shame in us which can attach to us forever*. What we may not realize is that shame is a major root-problem of addictive behaviors. So if we grow up feeling ashamed of who we are and what we are facing in life, it becomes difficult to embrace our life lessons without feeling deficient, or getting stuck in the woundedness of that experience. This sense of being stuck or frozen then limits our ability to grow, be present, or totally experience life in general.

In order for us to grow from life's lessons and not stay stuck, it is required that we shift from this judgment based process, to one that incorporates the second teaching of *In Lak'ech,* or paying attention to life's experiences as lessons just as they are; paying attention to our journey in life, to our experiences, and to the sum total of lessons that have been presented to us *without judging them*. The critical aspect of this process is learning to do this without judgment or criticism. This teaching also includes paying attention to the lessons that are brought to us by others, starting with our family. It is usually family and close relations that are our first teachers, and where the first challenges of these teachings take place. For each of us, it begins with being *acknowledged* for who we are, and given the ability to grow into our sacred purpose.

In traditional times, in preparation for one's life's journey, the elders would observe (pay attention) to the spirit (*tonal*) of each child as they came into the world to identify their guiding characteristics. Some traditions even begin this process before the baby is born. Mothers often share that they can feel the spirit of the child that they are carrying during pregnancy, and how each child feels different. By way of this process, in certain cultures, elders would ascertain and then bestow specific spirit names to each child. These spirit names were often connected to an animal or ancestor spirit. They would say, "This is a bear child or an eagle child," or "This child is connected to the deer spirit or this child has an old spirit like a wise owl." What were those elders really doing?

The wise elders understood that children have a *tonal*, or unique spirit. In western society, this is recognized as a person's personality, but the spirit of a person encompasses much more. For example, my animal spirit is that of a bird, an eagle. And that is why a lot of what I do comes in the form of squawking, talking, or speaking. As an instructor and therapist, I speak all over the country and that is part of my sacred purpose; it's what I do. But in order to stay in balance, a deeper part of the teaching for me is to recognize that birds can take flight (mentally, intellectually) for too long and lose their grounded-ness, so I have to continually pay attention and stay connected with earth centered people and processes so I can remain grounded. We each have our own personal spirit or character way. The challenging thing is that parents, with such pressure to raise children, prepare them for the future, and make them "successful," often don't take the time or have the time to see *who* their children really are before they begin molding them into some preconception of who they think they should be. We often expect our children to act and see life in a similar way, or style, as we do. We expect them to see the world as we do and deal with life in a similar manner.

My first son, Marcos, has somewhat of a bird spirit, similar to mine. He is outgoing, talkative, silly, and always very expressive. So when he was a child, it was fairly easy for me to *see the mirror of me in him* (accept him without judgment) and understand his behavior, because it was similar to mine. I could very easily see from his outward expressions what Marcos was going through, dealing with and conveying, because he was a lot like me. Even when he didn't express it in words, I could see or discern what he expressed in his movements. As a bird spirit myself, that was very much in line with what I was used to, and so it was comfortable and came naturally.

We tend to be able to flow with, and view as positive, the characteristics that are familiar to us. This is also the issue many times with ethnically rooted children in the western educational system and world, because they don't fit the culturally dominant mold of seeing, feeling, learning and/or healing. The dilemma is that in order for diverse, culturally rooted children to "do well" in school, they have to conform to the western system of seeing the world. This often creates a conflict between a child being true to their spirit and their culture, and doing well in school. The children that don't conform may have difficulty in school, and sometimes in life. At a minimum, it causes confusion within the child's spirit about them being accepted without judgment for who they are, and appreciated with their ethnic, cultural teachings.

Although important, in day-to-day life, this is not always easy to do. After having our son, the Creator sent us the blessing of a daughter, Renee. Her spirit was very different. Unlike her brother, she was not a bird spirit at all, and not immediately, outwardly expressive. What I realized was that Renee had a different spirit, more like a turtle. Although in all honesty, I didn't realize that at the time. Her spirit was that of someone that moved in a more contemplative manner. She would put her dollies in order, at the age of three. She also kept a lot of her thoughts and feelings to herself and that was challenging for me, as a bird spirit, to understand.

When Renee and I would get into disagreements, it created a dilemma for me. My bird spirit and therapist/counselor nature wanted to talk it out. I would say, "Come on Renee, let's talk about it. What's going on? Why are you upset?" And she wouldn't say anything. Seeking to get her to be expressive and explore some resolution, I would press on, "Renee let's discuss this. I want to solve this matter." Of course beyond my natural, bird spirit tendencies, that's what I was taught to do as a therapist. Yet, the more that I would press her to talk, the more she would draw further into her turtle spirit shell. "Come on Renee. Let's deal with this. Come on. I don't want us to stay upset. I don't want to hold this any longer. Let's just discuss this and deal with it."

I remember at times I would even take it personally, thinking that she was acting this way to upset me, and to reject me. But the more that I would press her, the further she would go into her shell. In retrospect, I have come to understand that as the parent, I had the power to control the process and wielded the potential to make her feel bad; and define, in a negative way, how she was responding. What I was doing was not acknowledging or paying attention to who she really was, but reacting and judging based on my expectations of who she was. I could have made her feel bad about withdrawing. I easily could have gone farther along a potentially damaging path and asked her, "What's the matter with you? Why are you shutting down? Why don't you want a relationship with me?" And in the process, I could have even made her feel bad for instinctively being who she was, or acting in accordance with her sacred, turtle spirit and sacred purpose.

As fate would have it, *In Lak'ech*, or that reflective mirror of my daughter, challenged me. It called on me to pay attention to the lesson at hand, which was, first of all, my relationship with my daughter and honoring who she was. I had to get out of the way of who I thought I should be as the father and who I thought she should be as a daughter, or my expectations as the parent, or past experiences (wounds or baggage) as a child myself. These teachings challenged me to truly be present, so I could begin paying attention, and accept who my daughter was, as her true self. Especially as the father and the parent, I needed to pay attention to my daughter's sacred spirit, and the lesson and teaching she had for me; as opposed to my expectations at the time. In that moment she was my *In Lak'ech*, the reflective mirror that gave me the opportunity to go deeper and get closer to my sacred purpose through my role as her father; and also to be a clear, reflective teacher for her.

In order to reach this point, I had to begin paying attention to my own issues as well - becoming able and willing to separate my issues and lessons from what she had to teach me. What it meant for this bird-spirit father, was that I often had to sit and wait by my turtle-spirited daughter until she felt safe enough to come out of her shell. Another thing I learned about my daughter, who is now 33, is that sometimes turtles go inside their shell to resolve situations and never share them with anyone. This is a difficult thing to accept for a bird spirit who likes to resolve everything on the outside and see it clearly. So by paying attention to who Renee was, I realized she wasn't intentionally trying to push against me, or becoming introverted as a way to avoid dealing with the issue. She was just being true to *her own sacred purpose* in life. Eventually as time went on, it also became important for her to have the option of not going inside and speaking her truth, but that took time. In fact, only after she felt really comfortable with who she was, did she feel safe to do this and become her complete self.

RELEASING GENERATIONAL WOUNDS AND PATTERNS

"There are wounds that never show on the body, that are deeper and more hurtful than anything that bleeds."

-LAURELL K. HAMILTON

Many of us didn't have the blessing of having parents that were able to take into consideration the spirits of all their children, especially in the midst of the pressures of modern society. And to be honest, I didn't always handle situations with my own children all that well either. In fact, if you had parents anything like mine, they were focused more on survival, keeping a roof over our head, keeping us fed and avoiding their own fears of failure (shame) as parents. For them, the most they could do was be present and pay attention to our day-to-day needs, which often didn't include our spirit or our feelings. It's also important to recognize that some of our families carry generational wounds.

Some of our ancestors endured colonization, slavery, rape, torture and dehumanization. This kind of inter-generational trauma has had an impact on many of us, who we are as a people, how we live our lives, and raise our own children. I remember as a child wondering why one of my grandmothers seemed mean at times, or why my mom or other relatives seemed so rigid and inaccessible. I never stopped to consider that these behaviors might have come from a deep woundedness. For many of us, there is also even a genetic memory that may trigger behavioral responses to present-day discrimination, racism, and unfairness that unconsciously is the basis for the fears and anxieties of our family members and now ours as well. Moreover, inherited responses are reinforced in some communities based on the reality that disparity-related-stresses still exist. They fuel our fear and survival-based-responses in our relationships and in life.

In addition, these fear-based patterns may have been passed on generationally and definitely can affect the way you see yourself, interact in your relationships, and how you parent your children. As a result, if you had parents that were stuck in these fear-based wounds, then some of you may have developed processes that mimic these behaviors. Unfortunately, some of these patterns and stressors may have resulted in some of us going through a variety of hurtful and painful childhood experiences, the residuals of which we still carry. Living in a home with wounded relations often produces patterns where one becomes stuck in fear, insecurity, and filled with shame. For me, I remember as a child experiencing things that were very unsettling, as I saw my mom and dad do or say things to each other, to me or my siblings that were confusing and painful. I remember I would promise myself, that when I grew up I would never treat my children that way, or say those things to my children. Unfortunately, thoughts in our minds don't necessarily convert to changes in behavior.

In specific reference to teaching children to pay attention to their feelings, some of us also grew up in homes where our feelings or opinions didn't matter – i.e., "children are to be seen and not heard." We basically became products of what our parents wanted us to think, feel, and be. I'm not saying this was done in an intentionally harmful way and in fact, some of our parents would even say, "I'm doing this for your own good." Certainly, in their minds and hearts, they believed what they were making us do and become, was best for us. Unfortunately, parents in pain do not realize how these rigid patterns and harmful experiences can have a devastating effect on a child's true spirit, often causing one's true spirit to hide and sometimes get lost.

We raise and teach young girls from a very early age to be nurturers and givers. We give them dolls and say, "Here's your dolly, take care of your dolly, help mommy with this," usually some expression of serving or caring for others. We teach them to be compassionate, to give, give, and give, often without consideration of their own wants, needs, or feelings. In essence, we are teaching them to *not pay attention* to their feelings or true self. When these patterns are ingrained in a little girl, she may grow up becoming more and more estranged from who she is, or what makes her happy, at the cost of serving others. As she grows, it then may even be difficult for her to relax without thinking about what she has to do for others, or what needs to be finished to fulfill these ingrained expectations. These expectations get internalized to the extent that she may even become uncomfortable experiencing goodness or happiness, subconsciously looking for relationships or a partner that feed these unhealthy patterns.

In a similar fashion, we raise boys to detach in a different way. When they fall and cry we tell them, "Stop crying, don't be a sissy. What is the matter with you? Suck it up." We give them toys, cars and guns and we teach them to bang the cars up and shoot other objects, or even people. Although they may only be playing, play can turn into real life. Play is how children learn about the world. They act out emotions, experiences and actions through their play, often processing their internal feelings about their experiences through these activities. Watch a young child play with her/his stuffed animals or other toys and you can often ascertain how they have been treated. In the words of Peggy O'Mara, "The way we talk to our children becomes their inner voice."

Therefore, by teaching young boys to shut down their feelings, that their job is to play rough, and that they should deny their emotions if they get hurt, we are teaching them to *not pay attention* to their feelings or their inner voice. Consequently, when these boys grow up, they may have difficulty expressing their emotions, or being present at all, in their relationships. The deeper impact may be these boys having difficulty being expressive and/or committing fully in a relationship. This difficulty creates negative implications of hurt and pain with their partners and constantly feeling like a failure. Many men, later on, learn to mask shame and feelings of inadequacy by hiding behind excessive boastfulness, hyper-sexuality and excessive drinking or drug use. With this in mind, it is an important step for all of us to intentionally acknowledge and release harmful generational trauma and oppressive patterns that have been handed down, by incorporating some of the healing processes and ceremonies suggested in subsequent chapters of this book.

BARRIERS TO INTIMATE RELATIONSHIPS

We all come with gifts and baggage based on our childhood experiences or generational trauma. The questions become: "How can we learn from those experiences without being ashamed of the lessons? Are we willing to pay attention and face the mirror of these teachings in our lives so that past hurts don't interrupt our ability to be present in our relationships going forward?"

As a therapist, I have counseled countless couples who have ended their relationships because they got caught in old, generational patterns of reacting to each other's wounds, as opposed to working through each other's life lessons. The reason given by a couple for a marital breakup may be that the wife accuses her partner of being abusive to her, physically and emotionally, or his unfaithfulness to her. In addition, she expresses that in their 15 years of marriage, she never felt that he really wholeheartedly committed to her. So they end up splitting up and proceed to get a divorce.

The woman in this relationship believed that in getting rid of her husband, her problems would be solved. She moves on with her life and unfortunately doesn't pay attention, or do the *reflective work* of attempting to understand the patterns, and the lessons that came from that relationship. She didn't look in her reflective mirror, *In Lak'ech*, and allow time for her to release the patterns of pain while moving towards healing and learning. So she goes through a lot of grief, pain, shame and difficulty in the divorce. She even vows to never be involved with a man like that again.

The woman goes on and in about six months, she meets someone and finds herself in another relationship, believing that this man is very different and that he is nothing like the husband she just divorced. Well, you can predict the outcome because generational patterns are very powerful and we've all been there. Yes, unfortunately, a year down the line, she begins seeing in her new partner, some of the very same characteristics as her ex-husband. Of course, she is devastated, and blames all men for being jerks and blames herself for being a terrible judge of character. So, what happened here? How was it that she fell into a similar relationship even though, in her head, she knew this was not what she wanted?

It was obvious the woman realized her ex-husband was abusive, a very inappropriate match, and responsible for his behavior. Knowing this, how did she end up in a similar relationship? While she was upset with her ex-husband (understandably so) and blamed him for their failed relationship, what she didn't do was stop to pay attention to the patterns and lessons that energetically drew her to that type of relationship in the first place. Hence, the "type" of partner she chose next and the relationship they shared, led to many of the same outcomes.

"Blame keeps wounds open.

Only forgiveness heals."

-*THOMAS S. MONSON*

Realistically, in the struggle of day-to-day life, paying attention to our patterns and lessons in relationships is easier said than done. Especially when we go through situations that are very painful, all we want to do is end such relationships and move on. Or, we may get stuck in the victimization and spend endless energy talking about what the other person did to us, to anyone that will listen. Unfortunately, if we don't take the time to pay attention and learn from the lessons, patterns and characteristics that got us into our present situation and our part in that relationship, then we won't be able to change our patterns and heal the process. Worse yet, because we are so used to these ways, we may not even notice these patterns when they are staring us in the face. Often, we don't realize that the patterns have a long history that can be traced back to a person's childhood and may even be generations old. The residual trauma from these experiences can have long lasting physical, emotional, mental and spiritual impact.

As a young boy, I remember growing up in a household where there was a lot of chaos, violence, drinking, partying, and many intense energies going on at the same time. At times, it was scary for me. I found myself confused, with my spirit retreating. I would then try and isolate myself so that I couldn't be hurt. In counseling sessions, I've asked people their experiences during trauma or fearful times in their life, and some of them share with me a feeling of being on the outside of their body. In intense times, they even felt that their spirit was away from them in moments of extreme threat – that it was on the ceiling looking down on them while the trauma was going on. Medicine people in indigenous traditions say that when children find themselves in dangerous, unsafe situations where there is extreme fear and hurt, the angels or protective ancestors will grab their spirit and pull it away from their body (seeing yourself from outside your body), so that their spirit will not be broken. Then when the danger subsides, their spirit is returned back to them. The work then becomes putting it back together again. Unfortunately, many of us are so relieved that the crisis is over that we go on with our lives not wanting to look at the impact the experience or relationship had on us, and often do not spend the time doing the work to put our spirit back together.

The problem worsens when such deeply intense episodes occur and then they are not talked through or processed resulting in the energy of trauma remaining stuck in your body, in your cell memory and attached to your spirit. This may leave you confused, uncomfortable, and with a sense of anxiety or insecurity. Years later, you are left wondering why, on occasion, you feel imbalanced or unhappy for what seems like no reason at all. Unbeknownst to you, the unresolved trauma may still be lodged in your body, attached to your spirit and may be inhibiting you from truly paying attention and being present in any relationship. In indigenous cultures of Mexico, the medicine people call this **Susto.** In Western society, it may be referred to as post-traumatic stress. Across generations, we continue to see many men coming back from war or women living in violent relationships with incredible amounts of stress and trauma. Just as it is impossible to go into war and not experience trauma, living on dangerous streets exposed to gang violence, enduring a violent adult relationship, or living in a violent home as a child can prevent anyone from being totally present. Unfortunately, there are children that experience this in communities every day, and then have to go school without any space or place to process or release this trauma. Obviously, there is no way that you can be present and pay attention to every emotion that comes through you. Your spirit would die. Responding in self-preservation, what many times happens in our own journey and in our development, is that our spirit separates from our true self and we become afraid to feel or trust. We end up living a fear-based life, always fearing the worst. What's important to recognize is that for those of us who have experienced trauma in our childhood, a major part of our journey includes putting our spirit back together. The beginning steps of this healing and recovery process starts with having the courage to be present and choosing to pay attention to these uncomfortable teachings that are part of our sacred path. Paying attention to what we really feel, what we really think, and on a deeper level, what our spirit is sharing with us is that first step.

For all of the above reasons and more, this teaching of *In Lak'ech*, although simple in nature, can be very difficult to integrate. Without this ability to know and enjoy what we are feeling in the present, we cannot truly experience healthy relationships with a partner, children or with others, and fulfill our sacredness. This simple task of paying attention to what's in front of us, to our needs right now, connects us to our true *sacred purpose*. This also allows us to notice when someone is disrespecting us or treating us in a dishonorable way, pay attention to what boundaries we need to set, and gives us the courage to honor our sacred-self by speaking our truth.

IN LAK'ECH: RECOVERING YOUR REFLECTIVE TEACHER

The final element of this teaching of *In Lak'ech*, is recognizing that all of our relationships and experiences, especially the painful or difficult ones are teachers for us. This may seem confusing to understand. How can you be present and pay attention to your needs, while also dealing with the challenges and struggles that are unresolved. As my mom would say, *"No hay mal que por bien no venga."* This basically means we should recognize that even negative or painful experiences can serve us in a good way; teaching and/or resulting in something positive. However, this is only true if you can truly *transform* the life lesson so that it serves you, not keeping you stuck from going forward. The *In Lak'ech* process occurs in different ways throughout our lifetime.

Growing up, I remember becoming afraid every time I heard my dad open a beer. I wasn't sure if it was going to be a happy time or one that ended in craziness and violence. This nervousness happened *every time* I heard the pop of a beer open. As a teenager, I would trigger every time I heard someone open a beer. Some people sedate themselves (drink excessively) to deal with the anxiety. But once I became a parent, I decided I didn't want my children, or myself, to go through this experience and as a result, I didn't drink alcohol. Even though I received push back from certain members of my family and friends, we didn't have alcohol in our house - not at birthday parties, or family parties or other social functions. This was my way of taking a negative lesson and creating a positive result. This also gave me the space to begin processing and releasing the pattern of fear associated with my father's drinking, and transform that into a healthier family tradition. This is not to say that you have to go to this extreme with changing patterns, but there must be a shift to disengage the past wounded energy, and open space for light energy. By the way, I don't trigger when I hear a beer open anymore, as I allowed time and space to transform that experience.

As a parent and as a person, you have the choice to stay stuck in the woundedness or transform those painful experiences into positive life teachings. It begins with showing up, being present and choosing to pay attention to life's experiences, not as good or bad, but as reflective teachers. So, recognizing that these wounds have thrown us out of our true rhythm, how do we start this process of detoxifying our bodies and spirits from the energies of the wounds of the past? The *Maestros/Maestras,* or wisdom teachers tell us that the way to be in balance is to live in balance; to live in concert with the natural rhythm of life- the earth, wind, water, sun and moon. Rather than reacting or allowing circumstances to trigger and freeze us, we need to reconnect with the vibrations of energy that are *in balance* and that can heal us. Since imbalanced patterns affect us physically, emotionally, mentally and spiritually, our healing needs to transform all of these areas as well. We can begin by honoring ourselves. Amazingly, many of the healing elements that are good for us are in nature, and readily available to us.

Consider the following:

- **The sacred wind, our breath** - The effects of living in a fast-paced, fear based society results in us living on guard and not able to flow. This means that we don't do even the most basic process of breathing, freely. It is important to open up space for healing, by taking time to allow our body to sit, *breath* and pay attention to the blessings in our lives. Not breathing freely reduces the oxygen in our bodies and can have a devastating impact on our health, and our ability to even sit still or relax when needed. Take time in the morning, during the day, and before you go to sleep: Take 7 sacred breaths, breathing slowly and fully in through your nose, and releasing smoothly through your mouth. Incorporate this breathing practice anytime you feel anxious or disconnected.

- **Honoring that sacred ocean in us, the female spirit of the water** - Our bodies are made of over 70% water, so when we connect to the water, it energetically balances us. It is very important for us to drink plenty of water so that we can replenish and restore our tissues, as well as detoxify our bodies from the stress and past trauma that stops our flow. It is also beneficial to go in the ocean, a river or take a bath on a regular basis, allowing the water to bless us and heal us. When we do this, it is important to do it intentionally, with the goal of detoxifying and cleansing ourselves from past wounds and hurts, and reconnecting with the sacred flowing energy of water.

- **Staying connected to the earth** - We know that foods that come from the earth are the best for us; plants, vegetables, fruits and herbs are rejuvenating and healing. In addition, we should take time to have our bare feet and hands feel and connect with the earth. Our bodies vibrate at the same energetic rhythm as the earth and the more we connect with the earth, the more balanced we will be. Some traditions will place their forehead or hands on the ground, as a way of depositing the negative energy they are carrying into the earth so it can be transformed, in only the way a mother can do.

- **Say good morning to grandfather Sun every day -** It is important that we can take some time every day to be in nature and feel the sun, as it is a natural strengthener of our spirit and a source of vitamin D. By connecting to the light of grandfather sun, the light spirit within us will be fed. Bathe in the sun's light and wear it as a protective shield around you.

- **Honor grandmother Moon -** In addition, connect monthly to the full power of the moon's energy. The teaching here is to allow our bodies to rest, heal, and rejuvenate. It is also important to acknowledge grandmother moon's energy, every night, so that we can rest properly. That means turning off the TV, and not engaging in over stimulating activities before we sleep. This allows our physical, emotional, mental, and spiritual selves to become grounded. Many traditions and cultures also incorporate monthly ceremonies to honor the moon cycles, and connect with the blessing of her curative power. This alone recreates a natural rhythm and detoxifies us in a transformational way.

All of these considerations point to the need to commit to interrupting our wounded patterns, to acknowledging our past and present while reintegrating a process that flows with the healing and restorative processes, and becoming increasingly in tune with nature and the sacredness of life.

TRANSFORMATIONAL HEALING IN TODAY'S RELATIONSHIPS

"Suffering is not holding you, you are

holding suffering."

-OSHO

In our present relationships, it's equally important for us to begin paying attention to the feelings that we have ignored or repressed, and the feelings that get triggered through day-to-day encounters. It's now time to respect those emotions. It's time to rediscover them, to honor them, to feel them again and to learn how to heal, express and for some to release them. The first step in healing our relationships is being able to *accept* who we are today- to acknowledge and accept the relationships in our lives today as they are, without judgement. This doesn't mean you have to like all people or agree with them, but you do have to know the "truth" about who they are and who they are not. When you do this, it then opens up space for shifts and transformations in your relationships to take place. When you finally make this choice about the kinds of relationships you want to have, amazing things can happen.

I've experienced this many times, but one of the most impactful to me was with my own mother. You see my mom grew up in a little *pueblo* in Mexico. She was one of the oldest in her family, and she had the responsibility of taking care of many of her brothers and sisters. She had to make tortillas for the family every day, wash clothes, and clean up for many years. My mother basically had to give up her needs as a child for the good the family. In a large family, there was very little time to tend to her own feelings or needs. It was all about the family and about what they needed her to do, especially for the girls and for my mother.

Sometimes, in a family with many children, it is difficult to find time to pay attention to each of their feelings. They are usually just trying to survive. Especially in impoverished communities, where there is a lot of stress and multiple challenges, they begin to repress or ignore those things that don't serve their immediate needs. I witnessed this circumstantial dynamic occur for my mom. When she raised us, she was a great provider. She often worked 16-hour days. Still, upon arriving home, mom would cook for us and do whatever else needed to be done to run the household. Rarely did she ever express personal feelings, other than frustration or anger with situations or how we were acting, and rarely did she do anything for herself.

I always joked that my mom never slept because when I woke up, she was awake, and when I went to sleep, she was awake. Growing up this way created a dilemma for me because when I arrived to college, where I was learning a completely different way, past experiences of home life confused me. I was taking a class in child development and learning about how it is important for children to feel loved and feel praised. They did a little exercise with us and said, "I want you to reflect back on when you were a child and think about how many times a day or week you remember your parents telling you they loved you, and how many times they praised you." As I reflected back on growing up in

Compton, with all the craziness in the house, I couldn't remember them ever saying that to me, or my siblings.

It's not that my parents didn't love us. There was love all around us in other forms or expressions - through my parents working all the time and by way they fed us and took care of us. Despite all of the chaos in our home, there was love. I felt it, but I never heard it. I never remember hearing my mom say, "I love you" or in Spanish, "*Te quiero.*" I simply didn't grow up hearing those words.

It took participating in a college course that confronted me with a different family paradigm to begin thinking, "Wait a minute, why didn't she share that with me?" At that moment I remember thinking, "Well maybe my mom didn't love me, maybe she just did those things out of obligation." But I knew, deep down inside of me, that she did love me and so I decided that I was going to start sharing my love with my mom - telling her that I loved her. So when I would go home to visit, I would walk over while she was making breakfast (mom was a great cook). I would give her a hug and say, "I love you." And she would shrug her shoulders and would say, "*Ya, ya mijo. ¿Quieres comer?*" meaning: "I know, okay, do you want to eat?" She was really uncomfortable with me hugging her, or me sharing that I loved her. I thought maybe she would say it back to me, but she didn't.

For years this confused me, at times leaving me upset and hurt that mom denied me this affirmation of our bond. Through guidance by elders, some self-healing work, ceremonial prayers, as well as becoming a father myself, I began *paying attention* to my mom and learned to not take it personally any longer. I realized that no one had ever shared that love with her. An outward affection was not what my mother learned. I was amazed. How you can go through your whole life being a nurturer and giver, and never receive it in return? So instead of feeling bad because my mom couldn't share "I love you" with her son, I began to *pay attention* and tried to understand and *accept* who she was in that moment, without judgement. I came to understand that she shared love in a different way, in the way of her animal spirit. Her way of expressing love was in making tortillas and tamales, fixing my torn pants (mom was a seamstress), and just being who she was and telling her stories.

In a similar way to learning to pay attention to my daughter, who is a turtle spirit, my mom also had a defining spirit, and shared her love in a different way - her own way. I started paying attention to who my mother really was, beyond being my mother. While being a mom, the one who fed and cooked for us and raised us, I had to acknowledge that *she was also a woman*, a person, with her own spirit, her own needs, her own issues, and her own wounds. I didn't know or understand her journey, and may never truly know or appreciate her struggles. When I was finally able to pay attention to what she had gone through and sacrificed, and accept who she really was as a total being, something changed. I began recognizing the many ways in which love manifested through her, instead of taking personally what she couldn't do to meet my expectations.

I had to let go of the regret that I held about the way my mother raised me, which had me focused on the past. Instead, I began paying attention to the present, and accepting my mother as she was, right then. As if this realization was not profound enough, not long after I had accepted how my mom was and began focusing more on what she did that was positive, something remarkable happened.

It was a weekday afternoon and I took my mom to a presentation that I was doing. Of course, at the presentation I acknowledged my mom, introducing her as my role model; she was very proud. My rather diminutive mom stood up and waved her little hand when I praised her, as she smiled seeming very pleased.

After the presentation, we went to eat and then I drove her home. She was about 73 at the time. As she was about to get out of the car she said, "Mijo, just drop me off here at the curb in front of the house." While getting out of the car, she grabbed her purse and began fumbling around looking for her keys. I asked her if she was okay. Responding that she was fine, mom opened the door and began getting out of the car when, in a hasty manner, she turned to me and said, "I love you! Bye!"

She walked quickly away from the car, almost like she wanted to say it, but she was uncomfortable hearing herself say it. It was so different that it shocked me so much that I just froze. But then I thought about it and said to myself, "Wow." That wasn't my mother's way or the way she was raised, but as soon as I accepted her as she was, it freed her to transform. It allowed her to pay attention to what I needed, once again not only as her son, but as a man.

My mom had learned to do something that was not her usual way. It was her spirit *paying attention* to what I needed. But it was only after I paid attention and accepted her for who she was, that I was able to open a place in me and open a place in her, in which both of us changed. That is the power of *In Lak'ech, accepting your life in the present and paying attention to your relationships* as your teachers.

That is the significance of paying attention to who someone is in their sacred-self, acknowledging and accepting their gifts and their baggage, the duality of the darkness and the light, without judgment or criticism or expectation. Only then, are we able to live our lives by acknowledging and paying attention to oneself, and to those people and things that surround us.

When people can be present in their lives and pay attention to their own physical, emotional, mental and spiritual sacredness, it's easier for them to accept themselves and others without judgment. As mentioned earlier, nature can help us to heal and grow in this process, learning to appreciate life more. To wake up and be present when the beautiful sun shines, when the rain comes to bless the plants and see the flowers in a joyous way, this is an intentional aspect of healing and growing. It allows you to live life in a sacred way because you are now showing up, and you are paying attention to the beauty of life. And when you start to pay attention, the blessings that come are amazing.

You begin to see the blessings that the Creator sends you, the lessons that are there for you to grasp which allow you to see the journey that is getting ready to avail itself to you. *In Lak'ech*, the reflective sacred mirror, begins to show you your true path. The answers show up and the healing begins. The things that you thought were impossible, now become possible. The visions you thought could never be realized, are now within your reach. But it is only when you begin to *be present and pay attention,* when you realize that the Creator, angels, ancestors, and the universe are just waiting for you; waiting so they could reveal the teachings, the lessons, the helpers, the guidance and the strength that you need to move to the next phase of your life.

As we continue to move in the direction of recovering, uncovering and discovering your true sacred purpose, your spirit will come alive again. *Welcome, your sacred purpose has been waiting.*

CHAPTER 6

DANCING WITH YOUR FACE AND HEART

"LOVE recognizes no barriers. LOVE jumps hurdles, leaps fences, penetrates walls to arrive at its destination Full of HOPE."

-MAYA ANGELOU

As we approach this next teaching, we reflect back on the first lesson of *In Tloque Nahuaque*, or being present enough to honor our sacredness. We then moved to the second teaching of *In Lak'ech*, or paying attention to the reflective mirror of life's teachings - the recognition that everything that has occurred in our lives and all the relationships that we have encountered have had purpose. These first two teachings have prepared us for this third related teaching.

The third teaching is that of ***Ixtli in Yollotl, or of Face and Heart*** - the ability to live your life with a sense of face and heart balance. In this teaching, we discover the importance of seeking balance in our lives. This sacred duality is a part of daily life in every culture throughout the world. Again, in our modern, fast-paced society, it is a great challenge to truly move in balance. Many of us find ourselves stuck and not moving at all, but merely being in a sense of motion, i.e. going through the motions.

Sacred Life Teachings

Motion and movement, although related, are two very different processes. Often, we find ourselves in motion, completing our tasks and participating in life, but really, we are just staying in the same place in terms of our spiritual and developmental growth; following ingrained patterns in our lives, but not growing, not learning, not healing, and therefore, not really moving. This is exemplified when people feel stuck, unmotivated, or even lost. Society gives us certain hierarchical markers such as degrees and titles and materialistic measures of success like money, houses, cars, and other luxury items to falsely judge whether we are successful or not. The sad reality is that many people, who are successful according to society's definition, are not truly happy or balanced.

Circle of Sacredness

Indigenous cultures look at success in a different way, not based on a linear, hierarchical or materialistic standard, but more on a circular nature. To illustrate this paradigm, imagine concentric circles. The outer circle is our physical sense. The second circle is mental sense. The third circle is our emotional sense. And the fourth inner circle is our spiritual dimension. In the center of those four circles is where we find our sacred self, our sacred purpose connected to our soul.

What happens when we are stuck, or are in motion, is that we continue to go around the same outer circles, the physical and mental rings, without moving closer to our center. We know that if we continue doing the same things over and over again, we're probably going to get the same results – being caught in the same position around your circle, no closer to balance or to our inner sacredness. This lesson of *Face and Heart* speaks directly to the process of transitioning from being in that type of motion that leaves one stuck, to true movement. The goal here is to move closer to our true selves, to who we really are; closer to our own sacred purpose and authentic sacredness. It is this sense of Face and Heart that allows us to bring balance to our lives.

In cultures all across the world, they talk about a sense of duality. In the Taoist tradition, they speak of yin and yang, and in African principles, they follow the concepts of will and intent. Also, the African concept of *Sankofa* is being mindful of looking back on the lessons of the past in order to best account for the present and prepare for the future. In my traditional, indigenous teachings in the Nahauatl language, they talk about *Itxli* in *Yollotl*. *Itxli* is the sense of face that looks backward and forward. You may have seen it represented in Mexican or Latin American art or artifacts - a sculpture or painting with a dual face. Some people may think that this represents someone being two-faced, but that is incorrect. In indigenous thought, Itxli is a purposeful duality of face. One face looks backward toward the ancestral teachings and the lessons that have come into our own lives. At the same time, it incorporates a face that looks forward on our journey to fulfill our Sacred Purpose. This creates a sense of true movement that takes us forward with acknowledgment, understanding and acceptance. This enables us to truly live life in line with our sacred purpose.

The other side of the teaching includes being balanced with a sense of heart, which in the Nahuatl language is called *Yollotl*, or *Corazón* in Spanish. It is the sense of heart, an interconnected heart, a compassionate heart, that holds unconditional love - one that reaches within us to our true soul/spirit. If we look deep into our heart, we begin to hear a spirit, we begin to feel a spirit, and we begin to hear an inner voice that connects us to the true essence of not only our feelings, but to an ancestral wisdom. That heart is also connected to our sacred relationships- the relationships with God, nature, the universe, our ancestors and the people around us. When we live with an awareness of face and heart, we can then experience a sense of balance. When we move through our lives with a sense of balance, we're allowed us to grow and heal with true, interconnected movement. Thus, we stop repeating lessons or patterns that are wound-based. This is where the work begins. In order for us to have true movement with a sense of Face and Heart, there is work to be done to release the pain and fear-based patterns, and to create space to heal, grow, and develop.

WEEDING YOUR GARDEN FROM WOUNDED PATTERNS

We begin by "weeding our garden". It starts by weeding away patterns that don't contribute to our sacredness and our sacred purpose; those things that don't contribute to feeling in harmony with our journey in life. This also may mean giving up certain habits, coping mechanisms, or addictions that are out of line with this sacredness. What is important to recognize is that people from all cultures picked up wounded patterns that attached to their cultural traditions, which continue to throw us out of balance today.

For example, in my Mexican culture which suffered through hundreds of years of being conquered and colonized, many of us have picked up false, wounded patterns of patriarchy where we mistreat women, are unfaithful in our relationships, and drink excessively. These behaviors sometimes are referred to as *macho,* as being part of our true culture. *This is false.* These are behaviors that some of us have internalized from the woundedness. The true indigenous teachings are directly opposite.

A true sense of *Machismo* is about honoring all our relationships, being truthful, faithful and responsible. However, unless we are willing to recover the true teachings and break the cycle of the wounded cultural patterns, then the toxicity of the "weeds" will smother our continued growth and damage our relationships. The step of weeding is necessary because there is no way that we can genuinely connect to the sacredness in our lives while we are living painful patterns of violence, untruth, selfishness, self-medication, or relying on addictive behaviors to cope. If these negative patterns are well ingrained in your spirit, especially if they are generational, then one may require additional support (e.g. Alcoholics Anonymous, Narcotics Anonymous groups, healing circles of support, therapeutic counseling, spiritual medicine) to assist. If you are in this place, you may wonder where to go or if anybody will be able to help. It is said that when the student is ready, the teacher will show up. If you follow the first two teachings of showing up and paying attention, then the teacher and/or support will show up. Addictions come in many forms. Some people eat into addiction, some are addicted to television, porn, sex, work and especially in the case of women and other nurturing people, even overextending themselves to others (i.e. anything that distracts you from honoring your sacredness). This step of reversing patterns may take a significant amount of effort, but it can begin with just choosing to face our lessons. It's important to note that the patterns that we carry not only affect us, but our relationships as well. And if not healed, they will be transferred to our children and other relationships. So, if you choose to shift your movement, it will also impact your relationships. And let me warn you, if you begin walking in a way that honors your Face and Heart, you may receive resistance such as envy or jealousy from people that are used to you living in another way. However, if you stay focused, the blessings and support will come.

BREAKING WOUNDED PATTERNS

Obviously, there are many barriers that can get in the way, but I will review five major patterns that keep us from truly moving towards sustainable Face and Heart balance in our lives. These five harmful patterns become the stagnating factors that keep us stuck and repeating the same behaviors.

"BUT WHY?" SYNDROME

The first pattern is what I call the "But why?" syndrome. Often, when we reflect on what has gone on in our lives, and especially the painful experiences, we want to know why. Growing up, we question, "Why did my parents not love me enough? Why did they abuse me? Why did they neglect me? Why didn't a certain person treat me in a good way?"

In our relationships, we get stuck wondering, "Why did this person deceive me? Why were they unfaithful to me?" Although it's normal for us to question why certain things have happened to us, to get stuck there is unhealthy. Usually the "But why?" comes up even more in those of us that feel that we have been the best person we could have been in a relationship. We feel that we tried to be the best that we could in our relationships and in life, so why would someone treat us that way? We tried to be honorable and we don't understand why we were mistreated.

Especially when the abuse has come from a loved one, we try to figure out why this person did this to us. And often in trying to figure it out, we may wonder if we contributed to the abuse. Let's be clear: There is no logical reason why someone gets abused, and no matter what the victim does, it is never his/her fault.

In our partner relationships, many of us get stuck trying to figure things out. "Why? If I was so good, why? If I was so giving, why? If I was so trusting, why? If I was so loving, why did someone treat me so poorly? Why would he/she lie to me? Why would she/he cheat on me? Why wasn't my love enough for him/her?"

We also have questions like: "If my mother is supposed to love me, then why couldn't she share her love in the way that I needed her to share it? Why did my father abandon me?" We have all of these "why?" questions that take so much of our mental and spiritual energy, that we get stuck in our past. Our spirit gets stuck and is hindered from moving forward. In very difficult situations we even question God as to why something occurred in our life. Unfortunately, when we don't get a satisfactory answer in our minds, we draw our own conclusion, "It must have been my fault, or I must have been worthy of such treatment."

This is especially true when focusing on an unanswerable "why?" These questions keep us stuck with no resolution, because the lesson is not ours to figure out in the first place. It has more to do with the actions of the other person, not us. Even though hurt people hurt people, it is really their lesson because they committed the act. So for us to search in ourselves as to why another person did something, or why the events happened in a particular way, is a futile battle. We are actually carrying another person's baggage when we carry these type of questions as our own.

The truth is that while we struggle with these issues and questions, many times the other person that hurt us is off someplace in their next relationship or phase of life without a care at all about what we are still obsessing over. Often people don't even recognize the degree of pain that they caused others, and in actuality, never will. In addition, as we carry these lessons, it energetically blocks the other person from really learning their own lesson. So part of the first step in moving and creating more balance in your Face and Heart, is for you to *release the need to understand why.*

Release the need to justify or make sense of the experience. It's time to acknowledge it happened, see the lesson in it, and let it go. Besides, often there is no logical reason in the sense of fairness or balance, for certain actions.

"Excessive analysis perpetuates emotional paralysis. You cannot heal and resolve your emotional material with your mind. The mind is the great divider. Your emotional material does not evaporate because you watch it. You can only heal your heart with your heart. Your heart is the great connector. When it opens, healing happens."

-JEFF BROWN

Let me just say that the more that you can practice the first teachings of honoring yourself, being present, and paying attention to the gifts in your life today, the easier it is to release the "why?" If you water the gifts, blessings, and answers that you *do* have, rather than the questions for the answers you don't have, then it will free your spirit to move forward. Being able to release the need to know why can be difficult, so you may need help to do so. Later in this writing, I will share some ways to release the "why?" As a suggested first step, consider in your meditation or prayers to ask for help. Whatever your belief or higher power, God, Creator, Spirit Guides, Ancestors or whoever, ask them to take the "why?" from you, and the need to understand. Such questions, and the very need to know, can prevent or slow you from healing, growing and moving forward. It will keep you stuck in in a sinkhole with no avenue to get out. Let it go.

"Surrender to what is, let go of what was and

have faith in what will be."

-SONIA RICOTTI

ANGER AND RESENTMENT

The second barrier to sacred movement is *anger and resentment.* When things occur in our lives that cause us pain, sorrow, or shame, our spirit feels out of equilibrium. For example, in relationships, partners are told, "Well, if you would have been more considerate, or more attentive to me, or done things a different way, I wouldn't have done this to you." Nevertheless, deep down in our spirits, we know the truth. Whatever the justification given, even if your mind wants to accept the rationale that if you would have been different, then things would have been good, your spirit knows the truth. And in that confusion, when you don't come to a healthy resolution, your spirit feels uneasy, which breeds a sense of anger.

Anger is the frustration that we feel when we are unable to resolve and return to a place of truth and connectedness. Anger is often the mask for hurt, fear or feelings of abandonment or disloyalty.

Finally, unresolved anger can also breed resentment, which is energetic frustration resulting from wanting to right the wrong, and bring balance. Once again, it's important to note that when we continue to focus our energy on a past hurt or on unresolved wounds, we divert our attention from the lesson we need to learn. If we stay stuck in the pain or in the emotion of the unresolved act, then it blocks us from moving forward. It's okay to hold a memory of someone from the past, but it's up to you if you energetically allow them to take up space and stay present, even emotionally, in your current life. In addition, when we feel the need for another person to "understand" what they have done to us, or what has occurred from our point of view, then we feed the frustration that exacerbates the sense of being stuck. This then triggers the many other frozen emotions that we have repressed, and magnifies these feelings. For those of us stuck in this pattern, we often replay the scenarios over and over again in our head, emitting significant amounts of negative energy, and widening the disconnection from our sacred selves even further.

The sad part is that anger and resentment can change our mood, as it produces physiological changes in our body. They can change the way we look at life and have a major impact on how we treat ourselves and others. It can especially impact those of us who have unresolved childhood hurt, as it can trigger past trauma. Many times we are not intending to react, but the unhealed anger and resentment operates subconsciously, causing us to treat others in very disrespectful ways. When this happens for extended periods, we can end up passing these patterns on to subsequent generations.

Even though you know what it feels like to be yelled at, ridiculed, put down or whatever the wrongdoing, what was done to you will be channeled through you to others, unless you figure out how to release the anger and resentment related to those situations in a good way. If the anger and resentment intensifies, it can lead to a strong imbalanced compulsion for retribution. This then creates another problem, the need to inflict harm, or make others feel what you felt - a result that only changes your energy and creates a further imbalance within you. By following through with any of these actions, it becomes *you* now, not the other person, who is responsible for the negative karma. This cycle often manifests itself in our present relationships. I've seen relationships deteriorate where couples cuss at each other, call each other names and are very rude towards one another. They lie and sneak around, and it becomes part of their day-to-day life. That deterioration is really unresolved mistrust, anger and resentment from past relationships. It's not an easy thing, but it's important for us to be able to release these unresolved feelings or we will live a life of anger and resentment. Many times we allow the toxicity to grow because anger and resentment feeds past pain. Furthermore, although it doesn't make logical sense, there are people that have been in hurtful relationships who continue to keep in contact with the very same people that hurt them. While counterintuitive, one might maintain harmful relationships with people who have hurt them, not because those relationships feel good, but because they are accustomed to them. Then when a crisis occurs and they treat them the same way again, the victim becomes upset with himself/herself for thinking it was going to be different.

All of those interactions bring toxic energy and continue to hold the spirit of that person hostage, even though every time they interact, the toxic relationship triggers the very same feelings. These feelings can reside deep inside of them and sometimes can become a part of their cell memory. It can also affect them physically in their sleep, digestive health, and overall metabolism. They may only have to think about someone in-particular, to get a stomach ache, develop sudden back spasms, or tension in the neck. What this denotes is that the experience of this particular relationship has penetrated them very deeply. This also points to the need to express and release the pain which is lodged inside of them, before it causes chronic illness.

RELEASING ANGER AND RESENTMENT

"God sometimes removes people

from your life to protect you. Don't run

after them."

-RICK WARREN

So how do we begin this healing process? I offer the following to guide you through this process. Be aware that if there are generations of unresolved anger and resentment present, it may take a while to fully detoxify yourself from this energetic connection but it's important to start.

If you are going to do this in a good way, you should set aside at least 1 to 2 hours for this ceremonial process. If you feel better having support, you may ask someone that you implicitly trust to be with you in the process. If not, you may do it on your own and/or ask your ancestors or a special ancestor to join and guide you spiritually. Plan to do this in a ceremonial way, with the intentions of goodness and healing (not with a sense of harm), and with the goal of becoming lighter and clearer in your life. If it is part of your ceremonial or faith practice, you can burn a candle, sage, copal, cedar or other herb to assist in the cleansing process. Either way, begin the process by taking a moment, taking a few deep breaths, asking for spiritual guidance and support, and attempting to do this in a good way.

The first part of this process is to write a letter to someone with whom you have unresolved anger and resentment. As you are writing the letter, jot your feelings down without any hesitation or censorship of language. Just write down what you would like to say to that person. Often it is not recommended to confront that person directly. Perhaps the person has moved on, or is not even alive anymore. Regardless, the true purpose of this process is for *you* to release the toxic feelings, not for the other person. So write this letter or speak it into a recorder, just to release everything you've ever wanted to say about how you feel, and how the relationship has impacted you. After writing that letter, create a small symbolic ritual where you shred it or burn the paper with the intention of letting it go. To assist yourself in releasing this toxicity, it may be helpful after you've burned or shredded the letter to incorporate a visualization process to move the negative shadow elements away from you.

You can do so by first settling yourself in a comfortable place in front of your altar, if possible.

- Take a deep breath in through your nose, hold it to the count of 4, and release your breath through your mouth. Do this 4 times.

- Now imagine yourself sitting at the ocean, or at a stream, with a bowl of water.

- Each time you exhale, visualize the negative feelings that you wrote coming out of you and falling into the bowl of water.

- As you finish with your words and your tears falling in this bowl, imagine yourself dumping the words and releasing the feelings into the ocean or the river, as you watch them float away.

- As you process this, make sure to breathe very deeply and allow the breath to come through you and out of you, cleansing your body of the angry and resentful feelings.

- With 4 cleansing breaths, give thanks and see yourself emotionally and spiritually free from these toxic feelings.

- Finally, make a commitment to stop telling this story of you as a victim, so that you can shift your energy past that experience.

Mayan glyph for noble speech

EMBRACING YOUR CULTURALLY BASED TRADITIONS FOR GROWTH AND HEALING

This practice of releasing shadow energy takes place in almost every culture around the world. The indigenous Huichole people of Mexico have a practice that allows them to cleanse in a similar fashion, journeying and praying every year on a pilgrimage. On this journey, they each have a piece of rope with them. As they walk, they pray on what they need to release that takes them away from their sacredness, sacred purpose, and sense of balance. With each of the things that brings up a negative feeling, whether it was about a person, something that happened to them, or even what they did to someone else, they tie a representative knot in the rope. The intent is to release these feelings or thoughts, no longer carrying these things inside of them. They walk and pray about this baggage until arriving at the ceremonial fire. On this day, so goes the tradition, each person offers these things up to die or pass. They then share with all those present, the things that they needed to let go, and throw their rope in the fire with the intention of releasing the toxic thoughts and feelings.

SHAME AS A BARRIER

The third barrier that blocks our movement and healing is *shame*. Shame is the result of growing up in a judgmental and guilt-based family, relationship, or society where we have been stigmatized for who we are, what we have done, or what has happened to us. Often times, oppressed, disenfranchised or immigrant populations have grown up with a sense of feeling "less than," unwanted or not wanted. They are made to feel like they don't measure up or that their gender, gender identity, culture or ethnicity is inferior by witnessing racial or discriminatory acts happen to themselves, their parents, relatives or people from their community. Science is also now recognizing what indigenous populations have known all along - pain and shame can impact you at such a profound cellular level, that the effects from these acts can get transmitted to subsequent generations.

Shame can also be very debilitating, and is a spiritual disease. It can energetically suck the life force out of you, and literally stop you from fulfilling your sacred purpose. Because shame grows a deep insecurity in you, it can keep you from developing or sharing your gifts and talents, for fear of criticism and judgement. This shame can also move you to even push away the blessings and opportunities that come our way. Shame is a reflection of the shadow side of others, which we often allow to influence our lives. Imagine standing in the sun and someone coming to stand between you and the sunlight, leaving you in a shadow. The person may be standing in your light unintentionally or "for your own good." Nevertheless, you don't feel the light. As an example of this, I've heard family members make fun of how someone in their family looks, or their weight, or even their tone of skin "in a joking way," thinking it didn't have an impact. But, it did. I've also seen a parent denigrate a child "to put them in their place," without realizing the harm she/he is causing. In the same vein, many women go through life, even from an early age, feeling ashamed of their bodies because of the disrespectful remarks or stares they receive. When it happens so frequently, one may even come to tolerate this behavior or accept it as normal, even though her spirit knows it doesn't feel right. In the worst-case scenario, she becomes accustomed to being in the shadow of shame so much that she believes that it is somehow deserved, and then begins doing it to herself.

Shame can also come from our own reflections or actions, which we have carried-out against others. This process of feeling uncomfortable (shame) for something we have done to ourselves, or others, is actually a good teacher. But if we internalize the judgement patterns we've learned from others, we can get stuck in patterns of self-criticism.

Shame also arises in us when we stay in relationships or situations longer than we should. Why did we tolerate that? Why did we go through that? After he/she deceived us and abused us, we stayed in the relationship and went back time after time. Why did we continue to take it? Why didn't we say something? We see here that unresolved questions, ("whys?") can contribute to feelings of shame.

If one continues to live in the shadow of shame, we get used to it as a normal part of how we think, feeling immobilized or frozen. In this situation, instead of the perpetrator making us feel bad, we do it to ourselves. This then gets integrated into how we look at and feel about ourselves, and about life in general. We may think that we're not attractive enough, that we need to lose weight, or that we're just not smart enough. When we carry shame for a long period of time, it can even become part of who we are energetically, and thus may influence the type of people that we attract in our relationships.

In many cases, shame can been passed down unintentionally from generation to generation, which makes it such a heavy burden. We may be carrying generations of shame on our backs without even knowing it is present. Maybe the time has come to release and let it go. The constructive question then becomes, "Can I change these patterns and shift this energetic burden that I am carrying?"

Another way to look at this question is to ask yourself, "Knowing that I am in the projected shadows and burdens that others have passed on, can I take the necessary steps to get into the light?" The real question is not whether you can, but *if you are willing* to do the work to step out of the shadow of shame and recover your sacred self again? The only answer has to be yes! Living in shame is like a slow death, or not really living at all. If not for you, the answer *must* be **YES** for subsequent generations.

> *"Our sorrows and wounds are healed*
>
> *only when we touch them with*
>
> *compassion."*
>
> -JACK KORNFIELD

RELEASING THE SHAMEFUL SHADOW

So how do we undo the feelings of shame? It begins by recognizing that regardless of what anyone has told you, whatever you have done in your life, no matter the situations where you stayed too long, or whatever other shameful behaviors you have exhibited because of shame; in the core of your spirit, **you are still sacred**. It is about knowing that regardless of the circumstances that have brought you to this shameful place, you did the best you could with the awareness, which often included wounds, you had at the time. Consider the wounds and whatever you have done to make you feel ashamed; the Creator has already forgiven you. God has already released those burdens, because the Universe, Creator, or whatever you call the Great Spirit, is a very loving, compassionate spirit.

Part of this cleansing is also having the willingness to release the shame others have bestowed on you, and shed the judgment that we place on ourselves for the actions we have committed. Of course, it's important to remember the lessons, to pay attention and look back, or reflect, on the lessons learned. That's why there is that dual face - *looking back, but not* **"Living Back"** (living in the past). You see, looking back is remembering the lessons and the teachings, which is important. However, there is no need to live back, and remain in the emotions of the past.

How many of us have been asked about how we grew up, or how we got to the place we are today, or even about an old relationship? As we begin recounting it, we begin to feel that same pain, anger, and shame, almost as if we were there and living it again (living back). When we tell the story, it feels like we are getting abused or shamed again. We may even begin to get angry again, or cry as we are retelling the story. It's important to understand that it's not necessary to *live back* the story or the situation in order to remember the lesson. We don't need to feel helpless, afraid or ashamed anymore. We don't need to stay in the shame or the anger and resentment. When we do that, it is almost like we are doing it to ourselves and reliving it again. It's important to remember, we are not there now.

"When it comes to self-trust, there is a powerful choice we must all make. As human beings, we often seem primed to remember who and what hurts us rather than focusing on how we made it through the pain."

-IYANLA VANZANT

FACING FEAR AS A TRICKSTER

This then brings us to the fourth barrier - Fear, the trickster of life. Of course, it's important to not be naïve, remembering the lessons, and not falling into the same patterns we have fallen into before. We can have caution, pay attention, and be a little bit more demonstrative of our boundaries and of what we need and want. These practices are really important, especially when we carry the old wounds and become slaves of our past burdens. But this can also cause us to become over cautious, hypersensitive, and reactive to everyday challenges in new and existing relationships alike. Many times, much of this is *motivated by fear* of being re-wounded or "failing" again. We may experience this when someone wants to be giving to us, or treat us with kindness, and we have difficulty receiving it; or when a partner wants to be loving with us, and we push their love away or avoid any opportunity for intimacy. It can even manifest in becoming suspicious of someone being kind or going out of her/his way to treat us well.

> *"If you live life in fear of the future*
>
> *because of what happened in the*
>
> *past, you will end up losing what you*
>
> *have in the present."*
>
> -NISHAN PANWAR

Fear based behavior can also manifest in one's unwillingness to complete tasks. We find students that only need one more class, or only need to finish a report for a class to graduate. They procrastinate on completing the task until it's too late. The ultimate fear can also manifest in someone sabotaging a relationship, just when things seem to be going well; or worse, being unwilling to commit fully. Infidelity, lying, and deception are all based on deep-rooted fear of intimacy.

Finally, because of one's fear of rejection, some people may go to the other extreme and find themselves going overboard in giving to others (e.g., buying numerous presents), smothering them with love, or on the other end needing to be constantly reassured of someone's love or commitment. Obviously, these are also attempts to mask the underlying fear of rejection.

This brings-to-mind when parents go overboard with their children. Many of us who have come from hardship or poverty remember the shame and humiliation of not having things or not being able to buy new clothes like other children. For some of us, that memory and pain doesn't go away. So, when we become parents and have the opportunity to do things or buy things for our children, we want to give them everything, whether needed or not, and often go overboard. Although a parent's generosity is important, when this is being driven by a sense of fear that resources may run out, or we may go back to where we were, then it can create another problem. In our children, we can end up creating a sense of hyper-generosity, entitlement or lack of appreciation. It is important to see the need for caution, especially if we have come from painful experiences in our upbringing or painful past relationships.

If fear is our motivation, then it is coming from a wounded place, which is not the healthiest motivator.

Of course, one may remain afraid to be hurt again and to repeat the same patterns, but one must understand that fear can be a friend or an enemy. Fear is not always a bad thing. As an example, imagine a child that is playing with a ball in front of the house and the ball goes into the street. The child goes to get the ball while a car is coming when, all the sudden, a protective spirit grabs that child and instinctively holds him/her from crossing the street. At that point, although the child is now afraid, fear has been the child's friend. Fear led the child to pay attention, and held her/him from going into danger. If the next day, the child goes to pick up the ball and remembers the incident but no longer wants to play ball, or looks at a parked car and gets nervous, then fear has become the child's enemy.

It's especially important for us to work through our fear as to not let our fears burden us or our relationships. Growing up in a dangerous neighborhood, I remember experiencing numerous fearful moments and situations. When I had children and they began to grow up, I found myself at times being extra cautious with them, even when it wasn't necessary. As teenagers, when they wanted to go out, I would remind them of the many things that they needed to do to be careful. One night as my daughter was getting ready to go out and as I was rattling off all the things she needed to watch out for, she asked, "Why do you need to put all your fears on me? Now I don't even feel like going out." What I had done in this situation was allowed my unresolved fears to burden my daughter, certainly unfair to her.

It saddens me that in my experience, I have heard people label an entire gender or group of people based on their own wounded sense of reality. As I was sitting in a restaurant one day, I heard a mother tell her daughter, "You just have to learn honey that all men are dogs, liars, cheaters, and assholes, so don't ever trust them." The ironic aspect of the situation is that then the girl's father came back from the restroom and sat down. Now whether the mother's personal experience with men was true or not, she had laid her fearful burdens on her daughter while disparaging the girl's father in the process. We cannot let fear become our enemy. It has to be a teacher to us. It has to be a constructive force that allows us to *show up*; yes, with our total experiences; to be able to *pay attention, be present*, and able to connect to the true teacher within our spirit.

> *"Too many of us are not living our lives*
>
> *because we are living our fears."*
>
> *- LES BROWN*

But as we walk down this path, there is one final barrier that seems to challenge most of us, at one time or another, in our attempts to truly heal. It is the big gorilla of the healing lessons: *forgiveness*.

"Forgiveness does not erase the bitter past. A healed memory is not a deleted memory. Instead, forgiving what we cannot forget creates a new way to remember. We change the memory of our past into a hope for the future"

-LUIS B. SMEADES

FORGIVENESS

The lesson of forgiveness is often one of the most difficult processes to incorporate into your life. Regardless of the offense, or the gravity of the wound, the act of non-forgiveness is like trying to move forward in your life with a bowling ball on your chest. Many people believe that forgiving someone means that you release that person from their responsibility of the act. It does not. It also does not mean that if you forgive someone, now you trust them, have positive feelings for them or want a relationship with them. But it is important to understand that unforgiven acts take up spiritual and energetic space within us, and in the end, make it very difficult for us to see and accept new blessings. If you can't open your arms or spirit to receive life's blessings because this big bowling ball is in the way, then you will stay stuck in your journey. When a past pain weighs you down, you can't truly *surrender* to the sacredness of your life. This burden can also destroy the present relationships you have.

With this in mind, I'd like to offer a 4-stage process that can assist in your movement towards forgiveness and releasing some of the other past barriers that were mentioned above. I will describe it first and guide you through it.

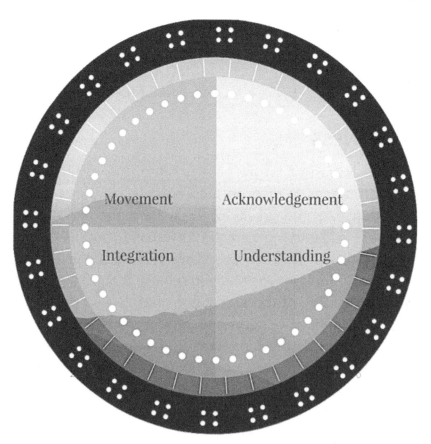

Circle of Healing

ACKNOWLEDGING THE FORGIVENESS JOURNEY

The first step in letting go of the burden of a past hurt, wound or disappointment is that we must *acknowledge* what went on, just as it happened. In order for us to do that, in healthy way, we must see the scenario from the outside, so to speak, as if we're watching a movie. This is important because we must emotionally detach from the incident and accept what truly happened as a fact, because painful emotion distorts reality. Often, we stay emotionally connected to the pain of an incident because we still can't believe it happened or really want to undo it. Natural questions include: "How dare someone do that to me? How could anybody do such a thing?"

In staying emotionally connected to the replay of the event, or series of events, we stay a slave to its painful legacy. It happened, there is nothing we can do about it, and we must be ready to turn the page and move on. This means transitioning from being the victim in the story, to being the storyteller - without emotion, without additional narrative, without the curse words, just the facts. And when something triggers old hurts, taking a few deep breaths and returning to the intention: *To release this toxin from our spirit, not to justify our hurt.*

UNDERSTANDING

For many people, even though the incident(s) could have occurred years ago, they stay tangled in the web of toxins from the incident by still attempting to figure how and why the offending party did what they did. In other words, they're still trying to figure out or *undo the incident*, which is obviously impossible to do.

It's important to accept that you will never truly understand the rationale for someone else's behavior. To emphasize the unrealistic nature of this wish, I offer a simple long-term observation: In my experience as a therapist, most times, the person who committed the act(s) doesn't know why. Especially if intoxication was involved, he/she often doesn't even remember the incident. So even if they tried to explain things to you, it wouldn't satisfy your need to erase the fact that someone disrespected or hurt you in that way. It doesn't make sense, and it will never make sense. The question then becomes, "Are you willing to stop hurting yourself by putting energy into attempting to undo something that occurred, or trying to figuring out why?" Accept that it happened, that you need to surrender to that truth, and move on.

"The truth is, unless you let go, unless you forgive yourself, unless you forgive the situation, unless you realize that that situation is over, you cannot move forward."

-DR. STEVE MARABOLI

INTEGRATION

The third step here is transitioning from the victim of this story, and other situations, by forgiving yourself as well. This means letting go of the negative self-talk about oneself, or the other person. This means being willing to integrate the process of *catch and release* into your learning. This means integrating what you learned from the situation, so you don't find yourself there again, and then release the story. Yes, this means you must commit *to stop telling the story* again as you recognize that it is toxic to you when you open that chapter again. Catch and release, turn the page and move on to a new chapter.

MOVEMENT

Regardless if your sacredness has been covered by grief, pain, abuse, neglect, shame, resentment or anger, it is time to uncover and discover what is inside of the sacredness of who you truly are. It is time to recover your sacred purpose so that you can change your world as you see it, and live in a sacred manner *now*. The following will guide you through a healing ceremonial process of forgiveness.

FORGIVENESS: RELEASING THE STORY

Set aside at least half an hour for this ceremonial process. If you feel better having support, you may ask someone that you implicitly trust to be with you in the process. If not, you may do it on your own and/or ask your ancestors or a special ancestor to join and guide you spiritually. Plan to do this in a ceremonial way, with the intentions of goodness and healing (not with a sense of harm), and with the goal of becoming lighter and clearer in your life. If it is part of your ceremonial or faith practice, you can burn a candle, sage, copal, cedar or other herb to assist in the cleansing process.

Take a deep breath and settle yourself into good intentions of releasing and healing yourself. As the narrator of the story, what you want to do is tell the story of an incident that still burdens you with just the known facts, trying not to get sucked into the emotions of the incident(s). After you have told the story while breathing deeply, sit for a moment and recognize that *you are you, in spite of the incident(s). You are in a safe place where you are at, and you are sacred just the way you are.*

To assist yourself in releasing this toxicity, it may be helpful to incorporate a visualization process to move the negative shadow elements away from you. So, let's begin:

- Now take a deep breath in through your nose, hold it to the count of 4, and release your breath through your mouth. Do this 4 times.

- Now imagine yourself sitting at the ocean or at a stream, with a bowl of water.

- As you breathe in and exhale, begin telling the story of the incident as a storyteller, with just the facts.

- Visualize, with every exhale, that the facts of the story that you are telling are falling into the bowl of water.

- As you finish with your words falling in this bowl of water, imagine yourself dumping the story and releasing the feelings into the ocean or the river as you see them floating away.

- As you're processing this, make sure to breathe very deeply and allow the breath to come through you and out of you, cleansing your body of the anger and resentful feelings.

- Now with 4 cleansing breaths give thanks and see yourself emotionally and spiritually free from these toxic feelings.

- Finally, make a commitment to stop telling this story of you as a victim, so that you can shift your energy past that experience.

This movement also has a second part to it and it is equally important. It is Self-Forgiveness.

SELF-FORGIVENESS: THE BIGGEST MOUNTAIN TO CLIMB

In the journey of life, we recognize that we are part of the duality of life. We are sacred, but also carry lessons that are the night and day. In other words, we all carry gifts and baggage. Contrary to what society or mental health practitioners tell us, we can attend as much therapy, church, or ceremony as we can, but there are still teachings, lessons, and struggles to work through. Ultimately, we cannot assimilate the lessons and make the changes needed within, without putting in the self-work.

"As we were finishing a sweat lodge ceremony, the medicine man said to us, 'Now the real ceremony begins: to do the work to live these teachings every day, in all your relationships.'"

-JERRY TELLO

Moreover, all of us have done things that have fallen short, hurt others, and hurt ourselves. Many times, these hurtful actions are the result of passed on, unresolved, generational pain through substance abuse, physical abuse, and toxic behaviors. They can also be the result of becoming rigid, critical, judgmental, and oppressive, based on our newfound "goodness/ holiness."

Whatever the circumstance, what lies at the base of relationship wounds is, many times, our inability to forgive ourselves for past transgressions. The problem becomes: *if we don't do this, we will never be whole.* As mentioned in an earlier chapter, the Creator, God, and the ancestors have already released that burden from us, but it is our choice whether we retain or release the guilt. Let me be clear. This is not justifying or rationalizing a harmful action, or saying that others will be able to surrender their issues related to the matter. However, it is important in our journey in life, to take the teachings of self-forgiveness from the experience and release the burdens that keep us from sacredness. Together with this process is our commitment to stay on the sacred path, and not return to the harmful ways. This means for some that we may need the support of groups (AA, NA, etc.), a therapist, or spiritual council on an ongoing basis throughout our lives to keep our commitment to these sacred ways.

Now, follow the same 4-direction process that we did previously to create a path for self-forgiveness and living the lesson of that experience in a sacred way.

ACKNOWLEDGEMENT

The first step in letting go of the burden of past wounds or transgression is that we must acknowledge what went on, just as it happened. Again in order to do that, we must see the scenario from the outside, as if we're watching a movie. We must emotionally detach from the incident, and accept what truly happened as a fact, as painful emotions only distort reality. Don't justify or rationalize the story, but see it for what truly happened.

Often, we energetically and emotionally stay connected to the pain of the incident, because it is often too painful for us to admit that we did such an action. We can't believe it happened, and rationalize it, "I did that because..." or, "If this wouldn't have happened then,..." As time passes, we also add our interpretations, thoughts, and characters to the story, as if they are facts. They are not. In staying emotionally connected or justifying the replay of the event or series of events, we remain a slave to its painful legacy. It happened. There is nothing we can do about it and we must be ready to face it, to incorporate the lesson in our lives and turn the page to move on.

This means transitioning from being the doer of harm in the story, to being the storyteller. So now try and tell the story as a storyteller without emotion, without the curse words, without justifications. And when you find yourself triggering, take a few deep breaths and remember the intention: To learn the lesson, but to also release this toxin from your spirit, not to justify your hurt.

UNDERSTANDING

For many of us, even though the incident occurred years ago, we stay tangled in the web of toxins from the incident by still attempting to figure out how and why other people stay upset or connected to the incident. This is especially true if you have repeated a similar infraction numerous times.

Sometimes, we just want them to "understand how and why this happened," or "what I was thinking when this happened?" - still trying to figure out, undo, or justify the incident, which is obviously impossible to do. It's also important to accept that we will never truly understand the rationale for our behavior.

We also need to accept that we will never understand the impact that our action has had on someone else. If we were intoxicated, then we may not even remember the incident. So even if it was explained to us, it wouldn't satisfy our need to erase that fact that we disrespected or hurt others in that way. It doesn't make sense and it will never make sense. The question then becomes, "Are we willing to accept the teachings and commit to do what we need to do, to accept responsibility and work on our issues?"

Stop hurting yourself by putting energy into attempting to undo something that occurred, and trying to figure out why. Accept that it did happen and that, in reality, you need to *surrender* to that truth and move on.

"The victim mindset dilutes the human potential. By not accepting personal responsibility for our circumstances, we greatly reduce our power to change. Being a victim of an unfortunate event should not be confused with playing the victim; the former was not your choice but the latter is your choice and, if you let it, it can become a way of life."

-DR. STEVE MARABOLI

INTEGRATION

The third step here is transitioning from being the perpetrator of this story, and other situations, by forgiving yourself as well. This means letting go of the negative self-talk about the situation, but more importantly, about yourself. Before you take this step, you may need to acknowledge and apologize to those people that you've harmed for the hurt you've caused. This is where you may need council to see if this is the best thing at this point in your life, and the life of others involved.

You don't want to bring up old wounds, but it may be enough for you to ceremonially acknowledge your action and commit to work on the issues that got you there. This also means being willing to integrate the process of *catch and release* into your learning. This translates into integrating what you learned from the situation, taking that knowledge so you don't find yourself there again, and then releasing the story. It means committing to no longer telling that story anymore, recognizing that it is toxic when you open that chapter again. Catch and release, turn the page, and move on to a new chapter. Let me note that although you may have moved forward with this teaching, those that you have hurt may still be stuck. And the best thing for you do is to live your sacred truth, and allow them to live theirs.

MOVEMENT

Plan to do this in a ceremonial way, with the intention of goodness and healing (not with a sense of justification), with the goal of becoming lighter and clearer. If it is part of your ceremonial or faith practice, you can burn a candle, sage, copal, cedar or other herb to assist in the cleansing process.

As the narrator of the story, tell it with just the known facts, trying not to get sucked into the emotions or justification of the incident(s). After you have told the story while breathing deeply, sit for a moment and recognize that you are you, in spite of the incident(s), and are *sacred* just the way you are.

To assist yourself in releasing this toxicity, it may be helpful to incorporate a visualization process to move the negative shadow elements away from you. You can do so by first settling yourself in a comfortable place, in front of your altar if possible.

- Now take a deep breath in through your nose, hold for a count of 4, and release your breath through your mouth. Do this 4 times.

- Now imagine yourself sitting at the ocean or at a stream, with a bowl of water.

- Visualize, with every exhale, that the facts of the story are falling into the bowl of water.

- As you finish with your words falling in this bowl of water, imagine yourself dumping the story and releasing the feelings into the ocean or the river as you see them floating away.

- As you're processing this, make sure to breathe very deeply and allow the breath to come through you and out of you, cleansing your body of the anger and resentful feelings.

- Now with 4 cleansing breaths give thanks and see yourself emotionally and spiritually free from these toxic feelings.

- Finally, make a commitment to stop telling this story of you as a perpetrator, so that you can shift your energy from the past experience.

As mentioned above, even if your sacredness has been covered by grief, pain, abuse, neglect, shame, resentment or anger, it is time to uncover it; to discover what is under there, what is inside of the sacredness of who you truly are. It is time to recover your sacred purpose so that you can change your world as you see it, and live now. No, not all the problems will go away, and not all the issue become easier to deal with. But it is more about how you see yourself, and handle the life that comes to you, that will determine your life's happiness.

"While I know myself as a creation of God, I am also obligated to realize and remember that everyone else and everything else are also God's creation."

-MAYA ANGELOU

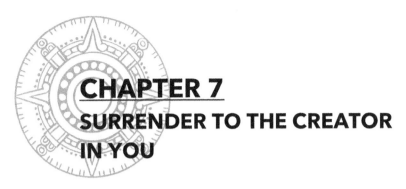

CHAPTER 7
SURRENDER TO THE CREATOR IN YOU

"Surrender simply means keeping

God's will before your own."

-RADHANATH SWAMI

As we move on in this journey of life, we begin to recognize that life is a circle. It is a circle that can bring us many blessings and many gifts. Life is also a cycle. I describe circles as those things that create true movement and connect us to our sacredness, and cycles are those things that stagnate and disconnect us. A cycle includes wounds and patterns that have come to us in painful or difficult ways, such as the cycles of abuse, violence and addiction. The circles are the elements of nature: the earth, water, wind, sun and moon that are always available to us; our positive ancestral teachings, values, traditions, and life enhancing relationships. What we must decide is whether we live our lives based on circles or on cycles. What we've explored so far is our innate ability, despite stifling cycles, to recover our sacredness and our purpose. For some of us, it is something we never even knew that we had. But for most of us, we have known that there was something deeper, something missing, something that wasn't quite complete or fulfilled within us. If you didn't know it before, you can now identify this missing element as your sacredness and your sacred purpose, recognizing that you are on your sacred path. Moreover, there is a reason why these teachings, that come from the creative force, are coming to you and why they have presented themselves to you now.

In all parts of the world, there are lessons and medicine available to us. It's always right there in our reach. But many times, we don't even realize it (pay attention). I shared a story earlier about a visiting Huichol elder who taught me a lesson about drinking coffee, and being present. There are many such stories and lessons that come to us in our daily lives. But if we are stuck in our cycles, we may not recognize them.

So now we move to the fourth lesson; one that is so significant for completing this circle of healing. It is the teaching of "Xochitl in Cuicatl," that of Flower and Song. This teaching points to us being able to surrender to the totality of who you are, past and present, and allowing your future to **flower in growth and sing in beauty.**

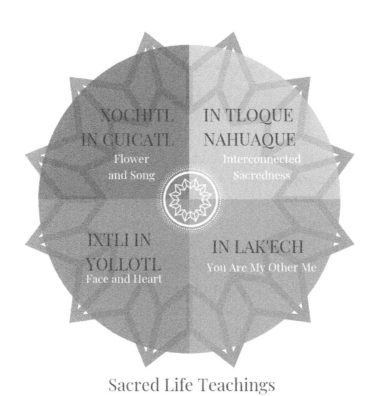

Sacred Life Teachings

This may seem mystical or a lofty ideal but as a child, I saw this happen in different ways: from my grandmother taking leftovers and making a delicious meal; to seeing my uncles take a beat up old car and making it into classic low rider; to us kids taking an old blanket and making it into a pretend fort for us to play. If we don't get stuck in the old wounds and the expectations of what we thought should be, we can create life from whatever has been presented to us that can flower beautifully and sing with joy. But it requires us to incorporate the next teaching of **Surrendering** to the Creator's plan. The practice of surrendering is one's willingness to give up our need to control life's journey, while knowing that there is a greater plan in place. In every culture, this teaching is presented in its own way in stories, proverbs, parables and life experiences. The following is one of those medicine stories that is shared in different versions, by people of various cultures, in their own way.

My daughter, Renee, says the teachings of various cultures are so similar because at one time, we were all one people and all the grandmothers were sisters. And the grandmothers got together in their different languages and cultures, and said, "Let's share these teachings with all our children." They might be explained in different ways because of customs and values, or because of the challenges and needs of different communities, but I believe that these teachings are mostly universal. Through storytelling, the ancient teachings helped to guide, correct and heal. Through them, the *"rites of passage"* (lessons of life) were conveyed and passed on from one generation to the next. This elder's lesson, which has parallels in many cultures, begins the dialogue and journey toward honorable and balanced living with a sense of *surrendering* to a greater plan.

> *"You need to trust to surrender, to ask for guidance and go within for the answers. All you need to do is ask."*

> *-KAREN HACKEL*

The Viejita (Old Lady) and the Four Values

This story takes place in a village where the people existed, living simply to survive. In fact, they were economically poor, agricultural people. The exception was an elderly man and his wife who owned an enormous mansion that lay on many acres of land. It had so many rooms, he couldn't walk to them all in one day.

The elder lived way up on a hill and had been married for many years. His lifelong goal was to have a good relationship with his family, which he accomplished. Then one day, his wife was called by the other world and left him. But before she left, she said to him, "Remember the promise."

The elder asked, "What promise?"

And she answered, "Remember the promise that enabled us to get this house and land."

The elder did remember that before owning this mansion, he was the gardener and his wife was the housekeeper. The way they acquired the enormous house and acres of land, was that the previous owner gave it all to them, based on one promise. The promise was that when they were ready to go to that "other place," and going to die, they would give it to someone who would continue to live in the same value-oriented and harmonious way that he saw them live. Specifically, the owner had said, "Remember, before you go, you have to give the house and land to someone who can carry out these *values* and make their partner happy."

The elder remembered, and he realized that his time was approaching. So, he called a meeting. Calling everybody to the circle he said, "I'm almost ready to leave and go to the next world, but first, I must keep a promise I made to my wife. I will give this mansion, this huge house, and its ten-thousand acres away."

In those days, the people didn't get a house or land unless someone gave it to them. The elder continued, "I'm going to give this house and this land to any man who wants it, as long as this person can tell me how he can create a harmonious life and how to make a partner happy. My life was devoted to my wife, so if you know as a man, how to make a woman happy, then you know how to live in harmony. There are four values one must live by. Now who among you wants to take the challenge of telling me the four things you must do, the four *valores* (values)? You must do it by the time the sun sets of the seventh day. Do any of you want to take this challenge?"

Almost all the men raised their hands and said that they would take the challenge. And so, the elder said, "There's only one thing you should know: Anyone who takes the challenge but doesn't come back with the correct four values by the time the sun sets of the seventh day, will die, and all his generations to come will have disease and suffering. Now knowing that, how many of you would still like to take the challenge? Anyone? Remember, this is a huge house with ten thousand acres."

Well, there was one man who thought he knew everything and could make any woman happy (As an aside, there are many men that truly feel that way. This is called ego). And this man shouted out, "I'll do it!" He said, "Hey! Four values? Make my partner happy? No problem! I'll get that big house, and the land, and I'll be all set."

This one man took the challenge. The elder sent him out and said, "Now go about the countryside and look for these values among the people, because the values are out there, but remember you must return by the time the sun sets on the seventh day."

Off went the man, walking and looking, and trying to think of the values. And he thought, maybe one of the values was to value money. But no, it couldn't be that. Could it be education? No, I don't know. And the harder he thought about it, the harder it was for him to identify the values.

As he was walking on this hot day, he became thirsty and went by the river where there were some children playing in the water. He stopped to get a drink, and seeing the children, he remembered that, being children, these little ones know our spirits. They are honest and say things we don't want them to say. They do things we don't want them to do, but they are so honest and clear with us. And the children, seeing this man, knew that he was searching for something, and they asked, "*Señor, Señor,* what is the matter? You look lost. Are you looking for something?"

And the man replied, "Ahh, what do you know? You're just little children. What do you know?"

A child responded, "Well, what's the matter, *Señor*? Do you need something?"

Then another one of the kids whispered, "Hey! He's the one! He's the one looking for the values."

Another child said, "You're the one looking for the values!"

Yet another child, "Oh, you're going to die if you don't find 'em and have disease, huh?"

You see, the children know. The children know when we're lost, and they know when something's happening to us, when we're searching. And they're honest, and open, and ready to give us their knowledge, telling us, "Oh we know, we know the answer! We'll tell you!"

The man answered, "Ahh, what do you kids know? You're just little kids."

"Well, we know what makes us happy!" the children said to the man.

"What? What?" the man asked.

"We like people to **love** us. We like our moms and dads to hug and kiss us. We like *love!* It's good! Yeah, that's what we like!" declared the children.

And the man answered with a sigh, "Well yeah, I guess that could be one of the values."

"Okay, bye *Señor!* Bye *Señor!* Hope you find everything you need by the seventh day, " the children said, adding, "cause if not, you're going to have disease and die!"

The man continued on his search, and a couple of days passed. He came to some orchards where farm workers were harvesting fruit and working the land. Seeing the good food, and being hungry, he asked one of the men, "Can I have some food?"

"You look a little lost and hungry, of course you can," the worker said, and gave some fruit to the man. The worker asked, "What's the matter, sir?"

The man replied, "Nothing, nothing. Ahh, I'm looking for some values but you poor men just work the land. What do you know?"

Then the worker, talking to one of the others said, "Ahh, he's the one, he's the one." And they talked amongst themselves, saying, "He's the crazy one, the one who's looking for the *valores*. He's going to get disease and die." And they began to laugh.

"I'm not crazy," the man protested, "but I *am* looking for the values. But what do you know about anything ?"

The worker replied, "No, no. We're close to the land and we know what's going on. We can feel when something's not right and you don't seem quite right."

And the man said, "But what do you know about values, you're just day laborers, poor people?"

The first worker replied, "Well we work all day long, every day, feed the world and all we want is one thing: **dignity.** Just for people to give us value for the work we do, to value who we are. We feed the people. We work hard just for one thing, dignity. That's all we ask. So there's a value for you."

"Ah, *gracias!*" the man said.

And now he had two values and went on his way. Soon it was the fourth day, then the fifth, and the man was getting a little nervous, starting to think that perhaps he shouldn't have taken on the challenge. He had thought it was going to be easy. As he came to the top of a hill, he saw a little house with a porch where two elders, an old couple, were sitting, drinking coffee, rocking and rocking, and talking to each other. The man, who was getting tired, wanted a place to sleep, so he went up to the couple and asked, "Have you any place for me to sleep?"

The old man replied, "We always have room for people passing. Where are you going?"

And the woman whispered, "He's the one, he's the one." And they began to laugh and said, "You're looking for the values, eh?"

The man answered, "Yes, yes, but I don't know if I'm going to find the four *valores* soon enough."

The old man replied, "It's very easy."

Hopeful he may have found another value, the man asked, "What do you mean?"

The old woman replied, "My husband and I, we've been married many years, 60 years, and the more difficult one is him!"

The old man looked at his wife, and said, "Ahh, she likes things in their place, just her way. We fought for years, until we learned to **respect** each other. And we've been together all these years, so that's the key."

So the man stayed overnight with the old couple, and realized he had learned a third value: respect.

But it was now the seventh day and the sun was in the middle of the sky and the man was back, walking through the village and getting very nervous. As he walked on, he heard a noise somewhere off to the side: "Psst, psst." He looked around, but he saw nothing. Then he heard the same noise again. "Psst, psst". Suddenly, he saw a woman calling him.

"Psst, psst." He heard again what he recognized as a woman's voice, "Psst, psst, come here!" As he drew closer to her, he saw that she was a very ugly woman with big warts. As he came even closer, he noticed how bad she smelled.

The man asked, "What do you want? I'm busy looking for some values."

The woman said, "So you're the one looking for the *values*, eh?"

"Yes, but (Phew, she smells bad!) what do you know?" The woman answered, "I've got it for you - I've got the last value!"

"But look at you!" he said with disgust. "You're over here, and you're all stinky and smelly, and what could you know about values?"

She replied, "Well, I sit here all day long. I see a lot. I know a lot. I see what shouldn't happen. I know what I didn't get. I know the fourth value".

"You don't know anything!" repeated the man thinking to himself that he was wasting his time with this ugly, smelly person.

"Well, it's up to you. If you don't get the value from me, then what? Disease, death? You want to die?" Said the woman solemnly.

The man responded, "No, but you're so ugly, and I…"

"Well it's up to you, go ahead," she said.

"Alright, all right, give me the value!" he retorted impatiently.

"No, no, no, no no!" the woman said. "You know nothing in this world is free. Life is a circle. I'll give you the value, but you have to give to me."

"But what do you want?" he blurted out.

"If I give you the value, you have to marry me," she replied clearly.

"Marry you?!" the man said. "Heck no I'm not going to marry an ugly, stinky woman."

"Well, it's up to you," she said. "Either you marry me, or you die. Which would you like?"

"Aw, you don't know the value anyway," he muttered.

"Yes I do."

"Well what is it?"

"Well, it's very easy," the woman said slowly. "If you want to make a woman happy, then yes, you have to have *love* like the children said, and honor *dignity* like the workers said, and *respect* like the elders said. But if you really want to make your wife happy, then you have to *give her her way*."

"What?" Asked the man. What kind of value is that? She said, "It's the value of **trust**. Trust is such an important thing and the reason I'm sitting here is because people have broken trust with me. Your *palabra, Señor*. If your word isn't trusted, then you have nothing."

"Ahh, give a woman her way, trust, that's a stupid value," he replied.

"But you have no choice. It's the last one, eh?" she said quizzically.

As the sun began to set, the man ran to the top of the village hill where he saw the elder smiling. "Did you find them?" the old man said. "Did you find the values?
The man answered, "Well, from the children, I learned about love."

"Yes, that's one."

"And from the farm workers, I learned about dignity."

"Yes, that's the second one."

"From the elders, I learned the value of respect. But I don't know about this last one." The man hesitated.

"Well, what's the last one?" asked the elder.

"Well, it's… it's giving a women her way, trust, and it's about giving your word."

And the elder said, "Yes, you got it! But where'd you learn about that last value?"

"Well, there's this old, ugly woman sitting on the…"

"No, no, I know about her! But how did you get it from her?"

"Well, I promised I'd marry her."

"Ahh, hoo hoo!" the elder laughed. "So then you will have to marry her, because you can't only *have* the values, you have to *live* them. It's not just about knowing the teachings, it's about living them."

The man looked at the house, and thought, "Well, it is a big house. Maybe she could live on that side and I'll live on this side. Eh, that way I don't have to see her or smell her?"

So they planned a wedding. The elder gave them the big house and the land. And the elder that night, because his job was done, passed to the next world.

The man and the ugly woman had their wedding. They invited everyone, and everyone came and celebrated the marriage. After the wedding, the couple went into their house and into the bedroom. There were many bedrooms, but they were in one room, and the man said, "Well, I'm going to another bedroom and sleep, and you can sleep in this bed."

"Yes, okay," replied the woman. "But before you go to sleep, give me a kiss goodnight."

"Do I have to?" he said with revulsion.

"Well, remember the values" she replied, "love, dignity, respect, and ...come on, kiss me."

"Do I really have to?"

"Yes", she said adamantly.

"Do I have to keep my eyes open?"

"Yes, you have to keep your eyes open so you can face your fears," she said, "just kiss me."

But he closed his eyes anyway, the man thinking that with his eyes closed, he would not feel anything. And he kissed her.

And when he opened his eyes, the woman wasn't ugly anymore. She was beautiful!

And the man said, "Wait a minute! You're not ugly anymore! What happened?"

She replied, "It's because you didn't allow fear to keep you stuck. You were able to get close to what you were afraid of. And when you got close to, and held what you feared, it wasn't ugly anymore. It turned into a lesson about something of beauty. But that's not the end of it."

"What do you mean?" he said.

She replied. "You have a choice."

"What's the choice?"

"Well, I can either be beautiful in the house, but ugly when we leave, or I can be ugly when we're in the house, but beautiful when we're outside. Which do you choose? Ugly when inside the house, beautiful when outside? Or beautiful inside the house, ugly when outside? If you choose beautiful inside, all your friends will talk about you and wonder how you could marry an ugly woman."

So what did this man do? What did he choose? He had learned something in his life. Well, what he did is what wise men do, and he said to his wife, "Whatever **you** want." *He Surrendered*. He allowed the spirit of healing, and of the Creator, to guide him. He gave up letting fear and ego control him, and him trying to dictate. He trusted his intuitive sacred spirit again, and surrendered the choice to his wife who symbolized the ancient grandmother voice in all of us; that voice connected to the ancestors and the Creator that oversees the journey, if we allow it. And with that , she was beautiful on the inside of the house and on the outside, because he had *surrendered* and truly integrated the four values of love, dignity, respect and trust into who he was as a person.

This important lesson of *surrendering* is the fourth teaching in Recovering our Sacredness and our Purpose. It is pointing to our willingness to trust what God, the Creator, and the ancestors have as part of our journey. This is a challenge for many people, especially because we live in a society that reinforces the importance of knowing everything, figuring it out and being in control. In addition, for those of us who have been wounded by lying, cheating and deception, trust may be extremely difficult. And for those of us who live with anxiety, a need to fix things, a need to have clarity and concrete direction, then this teaching may take some work. What we may not realize is that this need to control our lives and our uncomfortable lessons can even creep into our spiritual practices.

Incorporating this teaching even challenged me to pray differently. I used to kneel-down, or sit to practice my meditation and prayer. I would ask God for certain things, to help me with this, give me this, and take care of this for me. I still do a little of that but the majority of my prayer now is, "You know better than me Creator, God. Guide me. Heal me. Bring those people into my life that need to be there to protect me from the things that don't serve me. Please, show me the lessons and the way." It's often not an easy process to accept life as it is presented to you, because sometimes the lessons are difficult, they don't come in the way we want them to, or require blind faith.

We must truly believe, trust, and surrender the way the man in the story surrendered to his wife. The story symbolically meant that he was surrendering his spirit to the Creator, saying, "You guide me, you teach me." It is trusting that even what appears to be *"ugly,"* *like the ugly woman,* may be medicine teachings in disguise that will result in *flower and song.* And only if we are willing to embrace the lessons, will they become blessings, will the teachers show up, will the blessings manifest and the gifts become abundant. It's amazing because when you are able to surrender to the process, some magical things begin to happen. I know there are some situations that you've faced where you thought, "I'm stuck, this is horrible, and there is no way out." In fact, you may be there now. You may be thinking, "There is no way in the world I can figure out how to resolve this." There are things that you can't, in your wildest imagination, believe could be resolved or could happen, things that you think you could never experience and it may cause you to freeze.

We often think there are too many barriers and obstacles in our human minds, and too many things that we would need to change for us to get that result, and it's true. If you try and figure it out for yourself, try to move everything and solve everything yourself, you are right; it is too big for you to handle and change. But it's not too big for the Creator, the ancestors, the angels or whomever you look to as your helpers and greater spirit, to handle. It is within the teaching of surrendering that requires us to get out of the way and allow things to manifest. The more we trust the Creator and let go of control, the more the blessings will be able to flower and blossom, thus allowing our true spirit to sing in joy.

One time, when I was struggling with a troubling situation in my life and trying to figure out the best solutions to the matter, I looked at every possible angle and even called people to get their advice, still unsure of what I should do. And as I sat there praying and listening, I encountered a vision of a circle of my grandmothers sitting up in the ancestral garden where the ancients live. Sitting in a circle with their arms folded looking down on me, I heard them say, "Hey, we're right here. We're right here and have a better view of everything that's going on. And we have access to more resources than you do, but if you want to try and do it all by yourself, then go ahead, go ahead."

As I sat there, I just started laughing at how my mind needed to control, and think I was going to figure it all out, when in actuality, *I was getting in the way* of moving things to resolution. As long as I was holding on tight to the issues, I wasn't leaving any room for God, the ancestors, and my powerful grandmothers to do their work. In fact, the way it was resolved was not even close to what I was thinking, but much easier. The other lesson that I had to learn was to be patient, because in my need to want to fix everything right now, I wasn't allowing the universe time to move things into position to create the sacred solution.

Surrendering is not just a mystical process, but can have practical results. For instance, my partner believes she has "parking angels." She says, "Whenever I go someplace and need a parking space, I call on those angels, and they give me a parking space." I laughed and didn't believe her for a long time, but I have been in the car with her numerous times and every time, we get a parking space. You can say it's coincidence, but I like to take her with me as much as possible, especially when it's crowded, because we always get a parking space. And now I am a believer, and call on my own "parking angels" and they come through every time.

It seems simple, but that's just one example of the magic that can be manifested if you are connected, living these teachings, and surrendering to the positive spirit of the universe. I have also seen this spirit of hope bless my own children. I have seen magical, amazing things happen to them.

When my kids were young, they thought they were just lucky and fortunate. No, it wasn't just luck. It wasn't just coincidence. I realized that it was the prayers and practice of my ancestors, and those I offered, that had manifested in them as well. But it's in the surrendering, the belief in the gifts and the blessings, and the belief the Creator (angels or whoever you believe in), really wants you to be happy, that allows that process to flow; by surrendering to the sacredness in you, and the belief that you deserve to feel sacred. When you begin walking and *living* this path, you will feel something so amazing that will guide you on the journey to recover your sacred purpose and manifest *flor y canto*.

This does not mean that in surrendering, you will not have challenges or struggles. But it is how you see these difficulties and your ability to do your work, and then surrendering to the Creator's guidance, that will determine its movement. At the same time, let me share that I had a false perception. I thought as I attempted to live my life in a more sacred way, incorporating spiritual practices, there would be less challenges. And as a therapist and life coach, it was my assumption that the lessons were going to get easier for my own process because, of course, I am older, wiser, and have more teachings through experience. What I've found is that the lessons don't necessarily get easier, but now I am more open and present to recognize the teachings, the patterns and pitfalls sooner, and to enjoy the blessings.

I have learned to mostly avoid the toxic situations or people that are not good for me, and to ask for help when needed. This has allowed me to better recognize my reactive patterns sooner, rely on the positive teachings, and receive the goodness and the blessings that come in my chosen path as part of the sacred journey. I have also built up a strength, over time, that is a lot deeper, allowing me to face the challenges not as victim, but to see them as teachings. And when they get too big or heavy, I ask for help and trust that the support will be there. I recognized that the more I had a sacred practice that incorporates positive values, traditions and ceremony to amplify my sacred purpose, the easier it is to recognize that I am out of balance and to return to balance.

The act of surrendering is a process of embracing your sacredness and recognizing that you deserve to be happy: however, in-order-to get there, you must live sacredness as a daily practice. So let's try it.

CHAPTER 8
LIVING SACREDNESS AS A DAILY PRACTICE

"The secret to living well and longer is

to eat half, walk double, laugh triple

and love without measure."

-TIBETAN PROVERB

Sacredness cannot just be a prayer, an idea, or a spiritual ceremony. It must be a practice that you integrate into your daily life. Throughout this book, I have offered suggested processes to move you along your path that can be adapted and added to your own cultural and spiritual traditions. It will be up to you to choose what works and what fits best. I now offer a final overview to assist you in maintaining your connection to your sacredness, and embracing your *sacred purpose.*

IN TLOQUE NAHUAQUE: SACRED CONNECTEDNESS

This first sacred practice of sacred connection is taking time to honor the Creator, praying/meditating and connecting to your sacredness *every day*. Spend some time every day honoring your Creator, your God, that spirit in the universe. Do so in quiet, listening and paying attention to your inner voice. Part of that sacred practice should include some time in silence so that you can hear and receive the teachings that will come to you and those within. In connecting with the Creator/God/Spirit, you are really honoring yourself, reconnecting, and plugging yourself in.

To strengthen your daily practice, it's good to have a sacred space (altar) in your house or wherever you spend this sacred time. Have a sacred space that you use regularly, so that it collects this energy. Many people from various cultures also place sacred objects and sacred herbs that resonate with their personal spirit, that connect them to the genetic energy of their ancestors, in this sacred space. If you need ways to remind you to do this, you can also include pictures and symbols that help connect your creative sacredness.

FLOR Y CANTO: LIVING YOUR LIFE TO FLOWER AND SING IN GRATITUDE

Give thanks and have gratitude for what you have, not what you don't; for where you are and not where you want to be, or where you have been. Being grateful is a sacred energetic act. This practice is about watering what you want to grow. Obviously, the "shadow elements" and painful thoughts will come in, and sometimes life will seem like nothing but struggles. But if you take a moment every day to be thankful, and express gratitude for what you have, who you are, and for those around you, then joy will surround you.

As you incorporate this practice consistently, then it will gain energy and become easier in those difficult times to return to this energetic, spiritual space. In a society that focuses on material possessions, encourages always wanting more, and stresses preparing for the future, this lesson of honoring what we have is so essential. For that reason, it is important to let others know you're grateful for them. Give thanks for the universe, even the little things that others do. Spend some time being grateful for yourself, your work, and your willingness to look inside of yourself; to grow, heal, forgive and maintain your sacred purpose.

Aztec glyph "Xochitl", Flower

TODO SE PAGA: BE OF SERVICE AND ADVOCATE FOR THE NEEDS OF OTHERS

Serving others is a powerful way to grow, learn and heal. There is sacred medicine in service to others. It develops when you are doing for others, when you are helping others without any expectation of reward or acknowledgment. This is different than being a servant to others (I don't want to reinforce what we talked about earlier because many of us are incessant givers). After you take care of your own basic needs, do for others. Volunteer, advocate, speak up for others, help, share time, visit the elders, give of yourself, and just be of service, without the expectation of acknowledgement or payment. You will be surprised that in serving others, there is joy and healing that will be manifested. Make it a practice and a part of your life to devote service time whenever you can.

"Let us not become weary in doing good, for at the proper time, we will reap a harvest if we do not give up."

-GALATIANS 6:9

OLLIN: BLESSINGS AND ABUNDANCE

The Creator sends us blessings in abundance, and people to help us every day. Often, we don't feel like we deserve it. Or for some of us, it doesn't come in the right form, package or right person. It is amazing the different ways that blessings come. And it's interesting how we put limits on what we think we should receive. If you put limits on your abundance, that's what you'll get. Take off the limits, and recognize that there's nothing wrong with being blessed with goodness of health, positive emotions, and comfort. It's wonderful and you can feel good; it's okay.

You don't have to feel guilty about feeling good and being happy. It's wonderful to be able to have the things in your life that you need. There is nothing wrong in having things that add to your life, as long as you are sharing your abundance with others. What I have found is that the more that you share, the more you receive. It's the interconnected circle of giving and receiving, the Ollin.

The creator has provided all of the medicine for us to heal and grow in our lives. It has been here all along and the universe is open to provide everything and anything that we need, but we must be ready and open to receive.

IN LAK'ECH - TÚ ERES MI OTRO YO -
YOU ARE MY OTHER ME

We come back to *In Lak'ech*, the Mayan teaching that reflects the interconnected circle of life, *you are my other me*. In essence, the concept speaks to our fundamental interconnectedness. When you hurt, we all hurt. When you heal, we all heal. When you grow, we all grow. And when you get closer to your sacredness, we all get closer to universal sacredness. Peace in the world starts one piece (peace) at a time, and each of us has a part to fulfill. Make it simple, one breath at a time, one step at a time, and one day at time to move you closer to a life of blessings.

LIVING YOUR SACRED CIRCLE

"Intuition is a sacred gift you were born

with, innate in every cell of your being.

Follow it and allow your soul to carry out

your highest expression of life."

-MELINDA RODRIGUEZ

We all are born with a deep spiritual voice - that grandmother/grandfather spirit that gives us signals when things are right or not. Blessings are a part of life that we deserve. If we can heal and move forward with a sense of *face and heart* in balance, then we can find peace in ourselves. When we arrive, there is a sense of face that looks backward but doesn't live backwards; a sense of face that looks forward after having shed the need to know "why," releasing anger, resentment, and shame, and seeing fear as a teacher and not a bully in our lives. We must shed the anger and resentment, transforming the shame and fear so that we can once again live in happiness and harmony.

And finally, forgiving ourselves and others. The internalized sacred teachings also give us a heart that doesn't lead by fear, but is guided by faith. It is a heart that allows us to pay attention to our intuition and the spiritual, ancestral-voice deep inside of us. This allows us to continue along a path of integrity, hope, vision and the true fulfillment of our sacredness, allowing us to recover our sacred purpose.

The Creator and life's teachers give us opportunities and the medicine to release those burdens and open a path for us to step into a new day. Grandfather sun has shined its light on you this new day to water today's light in you. And I remind you that: today, right now, with all of your dark and light, the light lessons that you carry and the shadow lessons that challenge you, **you are sacred, you are a blessing, just the way you are.**

Remember, to live in this space, you must release yourself from the shame, judgment, fear and criticism, so that you do not allow others to disrespect you, or you continue abusing yourself.

> *"The greatest wisdom is simplicity. Love, respect, tolerance, sharing, gratitude, forgiveness. It is not complex or elaborate. The real knowledge is free. It's encoded in our DNA. All you need is within you. Great teachers have said that from the beginning. Find your heart and you will find your way."*
> *-CARLOS BARRIOS, MAYAN ELDER*

CHAPTER 9
LIVING IN GRATITUDE

My grandma would bless me every day and say, *"Que Dios te bendiga"* (May God Bless You). Every time my elder neighbor, Ms. Moseley, would see me, she would say, "Bless you, child." They were messengers of the Creator and ancestors to remind me of my sacredness, and bless me with the sacred spirit for those tough times when life became challenging and when I didn't feel sacred.

What I realized later in my life, was that these grandmothers didn't just get to this blessed place in their life, but that they had done their work so that they could offer these blessings to the children.

In a like manner, you choosing to incorporate these teachings will move you along the path to not only embrace your sacredness, but pass these blessings on to the next generation.

This writing is my form of service, of gratitude, as I am very grateful to have had wonderful teachers and life lessons. Although I still encounter challenges in my life, the difference is that now I realize that even the pain, struggle, shame and hurtful things, have given me medicine that I can share with others and deepen my own sacred purpose. If my journey and struggles were for no more than to share this with you today, and it helped you, and you can help one person, then maybe that was the reason for it all.

Life is not that of a hierarchical chart, or a straight line where you go from start to finish, winner or loser. Life is a circle in which we attempt to get closer to that sacred place of spirit within us, which connects us to the sacredness of who we really are. This movement allows us to fulfill our sacred purpose, complete ourselves with a sense of harmony and peace, collectively move to a better place, where our relations are filled with more light, love, integrity, respect, trust and dignity.

As we close this phase of your journey I leave you this sacred prayer/mantra that I suggest that you repeat as often as you need to:

I am sacred and part of the sacred We of the universe.
I have a sacred purpose that is essential and
interconnected to the universal sacred story.
I have sacred ancestral wisdom within me that guides and
can re-ground me throughout my life.
I have sacred medicine and blessings in me that can heal
others and myself, which I can share with the world.
I give thanks to the Creator, the ancestors, and all my
relations
Tlamish Tonatiuh (May the light of the Creator shine on
you always.)

- JERRY TELLO

GLOSSARY OF KEY WORDS, TERMS, CONCEPTS

Commitment to Sacredness -- Living in sacredness is living interconnected with all our relations and making a commitment to developing a practice of watering the sacred within. It is set on the foundation of a prayer of acknowledgement, of "I am Sacred, I am a Blessing;" committing to show up, be present, and choosing to practice those things that engender one's wholeness.

Disconnection -- Disconnection is the result of being out of balance with one's sacredness. As a society, we have come to approach the symptoms of disconnection and the inability to be present by sedating the symptoms. When someone is hurt, sick, depressed or just feeling sad, we medicate them; ostensibly, forcing that person out of being present with her/his feelings. What we don't understand is that the body, heart, mind, and spirit are magnificent teachers. Sometimes a person needs to feel down, in order to slow down and allow oneself to reflect, learn the lesson, and rebalance.

El Espejo (Life's Mirror) -- the lesson of *In Lak'ech* is one of *paying attention* to life as your teacher. This Mayan-based teaching of *In Lak'ech* (you are my other me) teaches us that everything in life is a reflective lesson (your other you). Within this ancestral teaching, *El Espejo, life's mirror,* is the way that life and all its experiences reflect teachings to us. Paying attention to life's lessons, to our journey and our experiences, is the indigenous process of growth and healing. The critical aspect of this process is learning to live this lesson without judgement, criticism or victimization.

Honor grandmother Moon -- Connecting monthly to the power of the moon's energy is essential. It allows our bodies to rest, heal, and rejuvenate. It is important to prepare nightly, so that we can rest and sleep properly. This allows our physical, emotional, mental, and spiritual selves to ground. Many traditions and cultures also incorporate monthly ceremonies to honor the moon cycles, and connect with the blessing of her curative power. This can help attune us to the natural rhythm of nature and detoxify us in a transformational way.

Honoring the sacred ocean in us, the female spirit of the water -- Our bodies are made of over 70% water. It is very important for us to drink plenty of water to replenish, restore our tissues, and detoxify our bodies from the stress and past trauma that stops our flow. It is beneficial to regularly go in the ocean, a river or lake to bathe, allowing the water to bless us and heal us. Do this intentionally, with the goal of detoxifying and cleansing ourselves from past wounds and hurt.

Inborn Sacredness -- Indigenous populations believe that children come into this world from the Creator and the ancestors as blessings and with a sacred purpose., They come into the world with a positive purpose that will add and contribute to the world in a positive way. According to ancient teachings, all children, regardless of the circumstances of our birth, are sacred and have a sacred purpose, and all people should be embraced in that way.

In Tloque Nahuaque -- In the indigenous language of my ancestors, the state of being connected to all the sacred, near and far, is referred to as In Tloque Nahuaque. It is the interconnection of a person to all that is sacred, or being one with God and the universe.

Ixtli in Yollotl (Face and Heart) -- Imparts the ability to live your life with a sense of face and heart balance. In this teaching, we discover the importance of seeking balance in our lives. This sacred duality is a part of daily life in every culture throughout the world. This lesson of *Face and Heart* speaks directly to the process of transitioning from being in the motion of survival that leaves one stuck or imbalanced, to true movement with balance. The goal here is to move closer to our true selves, to who we really are; closer to our own sacred purpose and authentic sacredness. It is this sense of Face and Heart that allows us to bring balance to our lives.

Itxli -- That sense of face that looks backward and forward. In indigenous thought, *Itxli* is a purposeful duality of face – a face that looks both backward toward the ancestral teachings, and the lessons that have come into our own lives. At the same time, it incorporates a face that looks forward on our journey to fulfill our Sacred Purpose. This creates a sense of *true* movement that moves us forward with acknowledgment, understanding and acceptance, which enables us to truly live life in line with our sacred purpose.

Yollotl -- (Nahuatl for heart [Corazón in Spanish]) -- The other side of the teaching of being balanced with a sense of heart. It is the sense of an interconnected heart, a compassionate heart that holds unconditional love - one that reaches within us to our true soul/spirit. If we look deep into our hearts, we begin to hear a spirit, we begin to feel a spirit, and we begin to hear a voice that connects us to the true essence of not only our feelings, but to an ancestral voice/wisdom. That heart connects us to our sacred relationships, nature, the universe, our ancestors and the people around us. When we live with an awareness of face and heart, we then can experience a sense of wisdom and balance.

Maestros/Maestras (teachers) - These are *"wisdom teachers"* who share the way to be and live in balance; to live in concert with the natural rhythm of life- the earth, wind, water, sun and moon; to reconnect with the vibrations of energy that are in balance and that can heal us physically, emotionally, mentally and spiritually.

Ollin -- the interconnected circle that gives and receives, which returns what has been given in order for the genetic memory of the ancestors, of peace, healing, and wholeness to continue.

Grandfather Sun -- It is important that we can take some time every day to be in nature and feel the sun, as it is a natural strengthener of our spirit and a source of vitamin D. By connecting to the light of grandfather sun, the light spirit within us will be fed. Bathe in the sun's light and wear it as a protective shield around you.

Mother Earth -- We know that foods that come from the earth are the best for us; plants, vegetables, fruits and herbs are rejuvenating and healing. In addition, we should take time to have our bare feet and hands feel and connect with the earth. Our bodies vibrate at the same energetic rhythm as the earth and the more we connect with the earth, the more balanced we will be.

Susto (State of Fear, Panic, Trauma) -- To be stuck in the pain and trauma of the past, and living life reacting to situations based on one's past, wounded self. This state of **Susto**, or being stuck in a trauma-based state, manifests in the inability to be present in our bodies, in our relationships, or be fully present in the most meaningful aspects of our lives.

The sacred wind: the breath of the spirit of the ancestors and Creator are essential to living healthy -- The effects of living in a fast-paced, fear-based society results in us living on guard and not able to flow. It is important to open up space for healing, by taking time to allow our body to sit, breath and pay attention to the blessings in our lives. Not breathing freely reduces the oxygen in our bodies and can have a devastating impact on our health. Take time in the morning, during the day, and before you go to sleep to take 7 intentional breaths.

Tonal -- the *spirit* of each child as they came into the world; identifies the nature and guiding characteristics of each person.

Welcoming and Acknowledging -- welcoming and acknowledgement of others as a blessing is the first sacred teaching in life. It begins with the communal act of acknowledging and accepting a new life as part of our relations, making it very clear that the child is *wanted*, and a valued part of the community.

Quotes

"I see a time of seven generations, when all the colors will gather under the sacred tree of life and the whole earth will become one circle again."

-CRAZY HORSE

"Suddenly all my ancestors are behind me. 'Be still,' they say. 'Watch and listen. You are the result of the love of thousands.'"

-LINDA HOGAN

"The circle has healing power. In the circle, we are all equal. When in the circle, no one is in front of you. No one is behind you. No one above you. No one is below you. The sacred circle is designed to create unity. The hoop of life is also a circle. On this hoop, there is a place for every species, every race, every tree and every plant. It is this completeness of life that must be respected in order to bring about health on this planet."

-DAVE CHIEF, OGLALA LAKOTA

"When a person feels SCARED, they no longer feel SACRED."

-JERRY TELLO

"To live is the rarest thing in the world. Most people exist, that is all."

-OSCAR WILDE

"You are either drawn by wisdom or pushed by pain. Either way, you will have to move."

-CAROLINE MYSS

"Movement toward your sacredness is the medicine that changes a person's physical, emotional, mental and spiritual well-being."

-JERRY TELLO

"Some people come into your life as blessings, some come into your life as lessons."

-MOTHER TERESA

"In the midst of turmoil and chaos, keep stillness inside of you."

-DEEPAK CHOPRA

"What are you reacting to? Ask Yourself that question every moment of everyday when your peace is disturbed."

-KENNETH WAPNICK

"Sometimes unforeseen opportunities emerge from the remnants of life's challenges. Sometimes it is possible to transform tough times into great growth and success."

-KAY DOUGLAS

"O' GREAT SPIRIT... help me always to speak the truth quietly, to listen with an open mind when others speak, and to remember the peace that may be found in silence."

-CHEROKEE PRAYER

"I love that this morning's sunrise does not define itself by last night's sunset."

-DR. STEVE MARABOLI

"No hay mal que por bien no venga" *(Even when something seemingly bad happens, goodness can come from it.)*

-MEXICAN PROVERB

"Meditation is not meant to help us avoid problems or run away from difficulties. It is meant to allow positive healing to take place. To meditate is to learn how to stop - to stop being carried away by our regrets about the past, our anger or despair in the present, or our worries about the future."

-THICH NHAT HANH

"Nothing is more powerful than a surrendered life in the hands of God."

-RICK WARREN

"People are sent into our lives to teach us things that we need to learn about ourselves."

-MANDY HALE

"There are wounds that never show on the body, that are deeper and more hurtful than anything that bleeds."

-LAURELL K. HAMILTON

"Blame keeps wounds open. Only forgiveness heals."

-THOMAS S. MONSON

"Suffering is not holding you, you are holding suffering."

-OSHO

"LOVE recognizes no barriers. LOVE jumps hurdles, leaps fences, penetrates walls to arrive at its destination Full of HOPE."

-MAYA ANGELOU

"Excessive analysis perpetuates emotional paralysis. You cannot heal and resolve your emotional material with your mind. The mind is the great divider. Your emotional material does not evaporate because you watch it. You can only heal your heart with your heart. Your heart is the great connector. When it opens, healing happens."

-JEFF BROWN

"Surrender to what is, let go of what was and have faith in what will be."

-SONIA RICOTTI

"God sometimes removes people from your life to protect you. Don't run after them."

-RICK WARREN

"Our sorrows and wounds are healed only when we touch them with compassion."

-JACK KORNFIELD

"When it comes to self-trust, there is a powerful choice we must all make. As human beings, we often seem primed to remember who and what hurts us rather than focusing on how we made it through the pain."

-IYANLA VAZANT

"If you live life in fear of the future because of what happened in the past, you will end up losing what you have in the present."

-NISHAN PANWAR

"Too many of us are not living our lives because we are living our fears."

-LES BROWN

"Forgiveness does not erase the bitter past. A healed memory is not a deleted memory. Instead, forgiving what we cannot forget creates a new way to remember. We change the memory of our past into a hope for the future."

-LUIS B. SMEADES

"The truth is: unless you let go, unless you forgive yourself, unless you forgive the situation, unless you realize that that situation is over, you cannot move forward."

-DR. STEVE MARABOLI

"As we were finishing a sweat lodge ceremony, the medicine man said to us, 'Now the real ceremony begins, to do the work, to live these teachings every day, in all your relationships.'"

-JERRY TELLO

"The victim mindset dilutes the human potential. By not accepting personal responsibility for our circumstances, we greatly reduce our power to change. Being a victim of an unfortunate event should not be confused with playing the victim; the former was not your choice but the latter is your choice and, if you let it, can become a way of life."

-DR. STEVE MARABOLI

"While I know myself as a creation of God, I am also obligated to realize and remember that everyone else and everything else are also God's creation."

-MAYA ANGELOU

"Surrender simply means keeping God's will before your own."

-RADHANATH SWAMI

"You need to trust to surrender, to ask for guidance and go within for the answers. All you need to do is ask."

-KAREN HACKEL

"The secret to living well and longer is to eat half, walk double, laugh triple and love without measure."

-TIBETAN PROVERB

"Let us not become weary in doing good, for at the proper time, we will reap a harvest if we do not give up."

-GALATIANS 6:9

"Intuition is a sacred gift you were born with, innate in every cell of your being. Follow it and allow your soul to carry out your highest expression of life."

-MELINDA RODRIGUEZ

"The greatest wisdom is simplicity. Love, respect, tolerance, sharing, gratitude, forgiveness. It is not complex or elaborate. The real knowledge is free. It's encoded in our DNA. All you need is within you. Great teachers have said that from the beginning. Find your heart and you will find your way."

-CARLOS BARRIOS, MAYAN ELDER

I am sacred and part of the sacred We of the universe.

I have a sacred purpose that is essential and

interconnected to the universal sacred story.

I have sacred ancestral wisdom within me that guides

and can re-ground me throughout my life.

I have sacred medicine and blessings in me that can

heal others and myself, that I can share with the world.

I give thanks to the Creator, the ancestors and all my

relations.

Tlamish Tonatiuh

(May the light of the Creator shine on you always.)

-JERRY TELLO

ABOUT THE AUTHOR

Jerry Tello is a father, grandfather, son, brother and relative of many. He is from a family of Mexican, Texan and Coahuiltecan roots, and was raised in the south central/Compton areas of Los Angeles. Over the last 40 years he has dedicated himself to the service of individuals, families, and communities. He has done so by speaking to over half a million people and training thousands of facilitators across the nation.

Mr. Tello is considered an international expert in the areas of: transformational healing, men and boys of color, racial justice, and community peace and mobilization. He is co-founder of the National Compadres Network and presently is Director of Training and Capacity Building. He has authored numerous articles, videos, and curricula addressing fatherhood, youth "rites of passage," culturally-based family strengthening, and healing the healer. He is the author of *A Father's Love*, a series of children's books, co-editor of *Family Violence and Men of Color*, has served as a principal consultant for Scholastic Books on International Bilingual Literacy curriculum, and has published a series of motivational health and healing CDs.

He has appeared in *Time, Newsweek, Latina* and *Lowrider* magazines. He is the recipient of numerous awards including the 2016 Maria Shriver's Annual Advocate for Change award, the 2015 White House Champions of

Change award, two California Governor's Awards, the Ambassador of Peace Award presented by Rotary International, and the Presidential Crime Victims Service award, presented by former President Bill Clinton and Attorney General Janet Reno.

Finally, in collaboration with the American G.I. Forum, Mr. Tello was part of an effort providing domestic violence awareness, healing, and support services to Iraq, Afghanistan, and Persian Gulf veterans and their spouses.

Presently, he continues to serve families and communities directly at the Sacred Circles Center in Whittier, California and is a member of the Sacred Circles performance group, a group dedicated to community peace and healing. He is the life companion of Susanna and proud father of three children: Marcos, Renee, and Emilio; and grandfather of Amara, Naiya, Greyson and Harrison.

Made in the USA
Las Vegas, NV
25 April 2022